98 Delicious Vegetarian Salads: A Cookbook for Healthy Eating

Spice and Everything Nice Hama

Copyright © 2023 Spice and Everything Nice Hama
All rights reserved.

Contents

INTRODUCTION 7
1. Mediterranean Orzo Salad 9
2. Roasted Beet and Arugula Salad 10
3. Broccoli Chickpea Salad 10
4. Creamy Pea Salad 11
5. Caprese Salad with Balsamic Glaze 12
6. Avocado Kale Salad 13
7. Kale Caesar Salad 14
8. Caprese Quinoa Salad 14
9. Beet and Carrot Salad 15
10. Cucumber Tomato Salad 16
11. Mexican Chopped Salad 17
12. Pea and Feta Salad 18
13. Bread and Butter Tomato Salad 19
14. Mushroom and Asparagus Salad 20
15. Roasted Butternut Squash Salad 21
16. Red Potato and Dill Salad 22
17. Zucchini Ribbon Salad 23
18. Roasted Sweet Potato Salad 23
19. Grilled Corn Salad 24
20. Roasted Eggplant Salad 25
21. Roasted Asparagus and Red Onion Salad 26
22. Cauliflower and Chickpea Salad 27
23. Lentil Quinoa Salad 29
24. Roasted Beet Salad 30
25. Broccoli and Raisin Salad 31
26. Roasted Sausage and Cabbage Salad 31
27. Farro Salad with Spinach 32

28. Cucumber Watermelon Salad 33
29. Roasted Cauliflower Salad 34
30. Avocado Spinach Salad 35
31. Arugula and Carrot Salad 36
32. Chickpea Salad with Spinach 37
33. Avocado Feta Salad 37
34. Artichoke and Olive Sala 38
35. Roasted Tomato Salad 39
36. Blueberry Watercress Salad 40
37. Tomato and Quinoa Salad 40
38. Kale and Avocado Salad 41
39. Spinach, Apple and Walnut Salad 42
40. Roasted Sweet Potato and Quinoa Salad 43
41. Zucchini and Sun-Dried Tomato Salad 44
42. Cucumber and Radish Salad 45
43. Broccoli and Red Pepper Salad 46
44. Arugula and Almond Salad 47
45. Red Potato and Green Bean Salad 48
46. Potato and Parsley Salad 48
47. Beet and Goat Cheese Salad 49
48. Carrot and Cabbage Salad 50
49. Roasted Pepper and Onion Salad 51
50. Lentil and Avocado Salad 52
51. Greek Quinoa Salad 53
52. Roasted Cauliflower and Feta Salad 54
53. Roasted Beet and Walnut Salad 55
54. Orzo and Pea Salad 56
55. Wheatberry and Orange Salad 57
56. Broccoli and Feta Salad 58

57. Roasted Sweet Potato and Feta Salad 59
58. Spinach and Orange Salad 60
59. Edamame and Carrot Salad 61
60. Pickled Cucumber and Tomato Salad 62
61. Quinoa Cranberry Salad 63
62. Roasted Root Vegetable Salad 64
63. Kale and Artichoke Salad 65
64. Barley and Sun-Dried Tomato Salad 65
65. Roasted Carrot and Parsnip Salad 66
66. Roasted Broccoli and Cherry Tomato Salad 67
67. Grilled Peach Salad 68
68. Quinoa and Black Bean Salad 69
69. Raw Kale Salad 70
70. Roasted Squash and Onion Salad 71
71. Avocado Tomato Salad 72
72. Green Bean and Potato Salad 73
73. Roasted Radish and Fennel Salad 74
74. Tomato Feta Salad 75
75. Radicchio and Red Onion Salad 76
76. Greek Chickpea Salad 76
77. Lentil and Spinach Salad 77
78. Broccoli and Sun-Dried Tomato Salad 78
79. Lentil, Artichoke, and Feta Salad 79
80. Roasted Chickpea Salad 80
81. Farro and Arugula Salad 81
82. Cucumber and Tomato Salad with Feta 82
83. Spicy Bean Salad 83
84. Quinoa, Avocado and Corn Salad 84
85. Kale and Edamame Salad 85

86. Asparagus and Pancetta Salad 86
87. Quinoa, Kale, and Apple Salad 86
88. Sweet Potato and Black Bean Salad 87
89. Roasted Mushroom Salad 88
90. Carrot Orange Salad 89
91. Grilled Zucchini Salad 90
92. Spinach and Apple Salad 91
93. Roasted Beet, Carrot, and Feta Salad 92
94. Mexican Quinoa Salad 93
95. Roasted Eggplant and Tomato Salad 94
96. Broccoli and Mushroom Salad 95
97. Kale, Beet and Cucumber Salad 95
98. Green Grape Salad 96
CONCLUSION 98

INTRODUCTION

Welcome to 98 Delicious Vegetarian Salads: A Cookbook for Healthy Eating! Whether you're a committed vegetarian, vegan, or just looking to add more plant-based options to your diet and lifestyle, this cookbook offers you a treasure trove of nutritious and delicious vegetarian salad recipes.

This cookbook features a variety of satisfying salads made with fresh, seasonal ingredients. Salads are proven to be a quick and easy way to maintain or improve your health and well-being. Eating salads helps to boost immunity and reduce the risk of chronic illnesses associated with poor nutrition. You will enjoy salads full of vitamins, minerals, and other phytonutrients from wholesome, plant-based ingredients, making them perfect plant-based sources of nutrition.

In this cookbook, you'll discover 98 salads that become your favorite go-to recipes. From classic tried-and-true favorites like Garden-fresh Tomato and Basil Salad and Garden Salad with Zucchini and Goat Cheese, to exotic delicacies like Tomatoes with Arugula, Sweet Corn, and Avocado, and Orange-fennel Salad with Figs and Arugula, meat-free meals become exciting culinary adventures.

We have recipes made with legumes, grains, and other plant-based proteins, making them not only healthy alternatives but also incredibly filling, satisfying meals. Whether you're looking for fresh and hearty salads to feed a party or shareable appetizers and snacks, you'll find inspirational recipes that serve your every need.

Delectable dressings, spreads, and sauces transform our vegan salads into incredibly delicious, flavorful meals. In these pages, you'll find brilliant oil-free salad dressings from Caesar-Style Green Goddess to Greek Yogurt Dill Dressing and the Easiest Creamy Airy Italian for a unique Italian-influenced salad dressing. You'll also learn to make tasty spreads such as Tahini Goddess Dressing with Apple Cider Vinegar and Molasses for a Mediterranean-inspired flare or Citrus Orange Dressing for a tart and tangy dressing.

Now is the perfect time to embrace a vegetarian lifestyle, and to discover how easy and utterly delicious it is! From simple one-dish salads to more elaborate salads full of ingredients and flavors, you'll find plant-based meals that will become the highlight of your day. So, roll up your sleeves and join in the quest for tasty, healthy, vegan salads!

1. Mediterranean Orzo Salad

This Mediterranean Orzo Salad is an easy and flavorful salad made with orzo, olives, feta cheese, artichokes, and roasted tomatoes. It's perfect for a light lunch or dinner and is also a great side dish.

Serving: 6
| Preparation Time: 10 minutes
| Ready Time: 40 minutes

Ingredients:
1. 8 oz orzo pasta
2. 1/3 cup pitted kalamata olives
3. 1/3 cup sliced sun-dried tomatoes
4. 1/3 cup crumbled feta cheese
5. 1/3 cup sliced artichoke hearts
6. 1/4 cup chopped fresh basil leaves
7. 1/4 cup olive oil
8. 2 tablespoons white balsamic vinegar
9. 2 cloves garlic, minced
10. 1/2 teaspoon dried oregano
11. 1/4 teaspoon salt
12. 1/8 teaspoon black pepper

Instructions:
1. Bring a large pot of salted water to a boil. Add the orzo and cook according to package instructions, about 10 minutes, until al dente. Drain and set aside.
2. In a large bowl, combine the olives, sun-dried tomatoes, feta cheese, artichoke hearts, and basil.
3. In a separate bowl, whisk together the olive oil, balsamic vinegar, garlic, oregano, salt, and pepper, until combined.
4. Add the cooked orzo to the large bowl with the vegetables and pour the dressing over the top.
5. Toss until the orzo is evenly coated with the dressing.
6. Serve warm or cold.

Nutrition Information (per serving):
Calories: 324
Fat: 16 g
Carbohydrates: 36 g

Protein: 10 g
Fiber: 3 g

2. Roasted Beet and Arugula Salad

This Roasted Beet and Arugula Salad is simple but bursting with flavor. The sweetness of the beets is a great contrast to the zesty garlic and lemon dressing, making it a delicious and satisfying dish.
Serving: 4
| Preparation Time: 15 minutes
| Ready Time: 25 minutes

Ingredients:
- 4 medium beetroots, peeled and cubed
- 4 cups arugula
- 4 tablespoons olive oil
- 2 tablespoons freshly squeezed lemon juice
- 1 clove garlic, minced
- Salt and pepper to taste

Instructions:
1. Preheat your oven to 400F (200°C).
2. Place the beet cubes on a baking tray covered with parchment paper and drizzle with 2 tablespoons of olive oil.
3. Bake for 25 minutes or until tender.
4. In a bowl, combine the remaining olive oil, lemon juice, garlic, salt, and pepper. Mix well.
5. Add in the arugula.
6. When the beets are done, add them to the salad and toss everything together.

Nutrition Information:
Calories: 175, Total Fat: 14 g, Saturated Fat: 2 g, Sodium: 117 mg, Total Carbohydrates: 11 g, Dietary Fiber: 3 g, Sugars: 6 g, Protein: 2 g.

3. Broccoli Chickpea Salad

With a delicious combination of both crunch and nutty flavors, this Broccoli Chickpea Salad is the perfect side dish for any occasion. It is an easy and quick to make, nutritious and filling salad!
Serving: 4
| Preparation Time: 10 minutes
| Ready Time: 10 minutes

Ingredients:
- 2 cups chopped broccoli
- 1 (15.5 oz) can chickpeas, drained and rinsed
- 2 tablespoons olive oil
- 2 tablespoons apple cider vinegar
- 2 tablespoons fresh parsley, minced
- 2 tablespoons slivered almonds
- 1/2 teaspoon garlic powder
- 1/2 teaspoon black pepper
- 1/2 teaspoon sea salt

Instructions:
1. In a large bowl, combine the broccoli, chickpeas, olive oil, apple cider vinegar, fresh parsley, slivered almonds, garlic powder, black pepper and sea salt. Mix until well combined.
2. Serve the salad chilled or at room temperature.

Nutrition Information (per serving):
Calories: 248 kcal; Carbohydrates: 23.9 g; Protein: 8.2 g; Fat: 14.7 g; Saturated Fat: 1.9 g; Sodium: 345 mg; Fiber: 7.4 g; Sugar: 3.8 g.

4. Creamy Pea Salad

This Creamy Pea Salad is a delicious cold side dish made with a mix of veggies, cheese and a creamy dressing.
Serves 8, | Preparation Time 10 minutes, ready time 10 minutes.

Ingredients:
1. 2 cups frozen peas,
2. 1 stalk celery, diced,
3. 2 green onions, chopped,

4. 1/2 cup shredded cheddar cheese,
5. 1/4 cup mayonnaise,
6. 2 tablespoons Greek yogurt,
7. 1 teaspoon Dijon mustard,
8. salt and pepper to taste

Instructions:
1. Place frozen peas in a medium bowl and allow to thaw for about 5 minutes.
2. Add the celery and green onion and mix well.
3. In a small bowl, combine the mayonnaise, yogurt, mustard and salt and pepper.
4. Pour the dressing over the veggies and mix well to combine.
5. Gently stir in the cheddar cheese.
6. Serve chilled.

Nutrition Information:
Per serving: 170 calories; 12.5 g fat; 5.5 g saturated fat; 10 g carbohydrates; 3.5 g protein; 370 mg sodium.

5. Caprese Salad with Balsamic Glaze

This fresh and flavorful Caprese Salad with Balsamic Glaze is the perfect way to make a summer meal light and healthy, yet incredibly delicious and beautiful!
Serving: 4
| Preparation Time: 10 minutes
| Ready Time: 10 minutes

Ingredients:
- 2 Roma tomatoes, sliced
- 8 ounces fresh mozzarella, sliced
- 2 tablespoons chopped fresh basil
- 1/4 cup balsamic glaze
- Extra-virgin olive oil, for drizzling
- Salt, to taste

Instructions:

1. Place the sliced tomatoes and mozzarella on a serving platter.
2. Sprinkle with the chopped basil.
3. Drizzle with balsamic glaze and extra-virgin olive oil.
4. Season with salt, to taste.
5. Serve immediately.

Nutrition Information:
Calories: 221, Total Fat: 13g, Saturated Fat: 8g, Cholesterol: 48mg, Sodium: 380mg, Carbohydrates: 9g, Sugar: 6g, Protein: 16g, Fiber: 1g

6. Avocado Kale Salad

This Avocado Kale Salad is a fresh, nourishing lunch or dinner option that you'll absolutely love. This easy salad is full of good-for-you ingredients, and is sure to give you a boost of energy. Serve this dish up as a vegan lunch, light dinner, or side salad, and wow your family and friends!
Serving: 4-6
| Preparation Time: 15 minutes
| Ready Time: 15 minutes

Ingredients:
- 2 bunches kale, washed, stemmed and chopped
- 2 avocados, peeled, pitted, and chopped
- 1/2 cup diced tomatoes
- 1/4 cup chopped red onion
- 2 tablespoons olive oil
- 1 tablespoon lemon juice
- 1/2 teaspoon black pepper
- 1/2 teaspoon sea salt

Instruction:
1. Place kale in a large bowl.
2. Cut the avocados into small cubes and add to the bowl with the kale.
3. Add the tomatoes, red onions, olive oil, lemon juice, black pepper, and sea salt to the bowl, and mix until all the ingredients are well combined.
4. Serve and enjoy!

Nutrition Information (for 1/4 of recipe):
Calories: 220
Carbohydrates: 12
Protein: 5 grams
Fat: 18 grams
Fiber: 8 grams

7. Kale Caesar Salad

Kale Caesar Salad is a light and refreshing way to enjoy a classic Caesar salad. This variation uses marinated kale for a full flavor. This dish can be served as a side or a main course for a healthy and delicious lunch.
Serving : 2
| Preparation Time: 10 minutes
| Ready Time: 10 minutes

Ingredients:
1. 2 bunches of kale, destemmed and cut into 1-2-inch strips
2. 1 cup of shredded parmesan
3. 1/2 cup of Caesar dressing

Instructions:
1. In a large bowl, mix kale and Caesar dressing until kale is well coated.
2. Top with parmesan cheese and toss to combine.

Nutrition Information:
Calories: 230
Fat: 18g
Carbohydrates: 5g
Protein: 9g
Fiber: 2g

8. Caprese Quinoa Salad

This scrumptious Caprese Quinoa Salad is a great option for a quick and nutritious meal. It is full of fresh flavors, wholesome ingredients, and satisfying textures. Serving 4-6, it takes 10 minutes to prepare, and is ready in 15 minutes.

Serving: 4-6
| Preparation Time: 10 minutes
| Ready in: 15 minutes

Ingredients:
- 1 cup uncooked quinoa
- 2 cups vegetable broth
- 2 large tomatoes, diced
- 1/2 cup sliced small mozzarella balls
- 1/3 cup thinly sliced basil
- 3/4 cup quartered Kalamata olives
- 2 tablespoons olive oil
- 1 tablespoon balsamic vinegar
- 2 cloves garlic, minced
- Salt and pepper to taste

Instructions:
1. Cook the quinoa according to package directions using vegetable broth.
2. Meanwhile, dice the tomatoes and slice the mozzarella balls.
3. Once quinoa is cooked, combine in a large bowl with the tomatoes, mozzarella balls, basil, and olives.
4. In a small bowl, whisk together olive oil, balsamic vinegar, garlic, salt, and pepper.
5. Drizzle dressing over the salad and toss to coat.
6. Serve and enjoy!

Nutrition Information:
Calories: 234, Total Fat: 9 g, Saturated Fat: 2 g, Cholesterol: 8 mg, Sodium: 332 mg, Carbohydrates: 25 g, Fiber: 4 g, Protein: 6 g

9. Beet and Carrot Salad

A fresh and flavorful Beet and Carrot Salad, this delicious side dish is easy to make and can be a healthy and nutrient-packed addition to any meal.

Serving: 4-6
| Preparation Time: 10 minutes
| Ready Time: 10 minutes

Ingredients:
- 3 medium beets, diced
- 3 medium carrots, grated
- 2 tablespoons extra-virgin olive oil
- 1/2 lemon, juiced
- Salt and pepper, to taste

Instructions:
1. In a medium bowl, combine diced beets and grated carrots.
2. Drizzle olive oil and lemon juice over the beet and carrot mixture and season with salt and pepper, to taste.
3. Toss the salad gently until all ingredients are evenly coated.
4. Serve and enjoy!

Nutrition Information (per serving):
154 calories, 9g fat, 19g carbohydrates, 3.3g protein

10. Cucumber Tomato Salad

Cucumber Tomato Salad is a refreshing and light summer salad, combining crisp cucumbers, juicy tomatoes, and basil with a light lemon-olive oil dressing.
Serving: 4-6
| Preparation Time: 10 minutes
| Ready Time: 20 minutes

Ingredients:
1. 2 large cucumbers, sliced
2. 1 pint cherry tomatoes, halved
3. 1/4 cup chopped fresh basil or chives
4. 2 tablespoons extra-virgin olive oil
5. 2 tablespoons freshly squeezed lemon juice
6. 1 teaspoon freshly ground black pepper
7. Salt, to taste

Instructions:
1. In a large bowl, combine the cucumbers, tomatoes, and basil.
2. In a small bowl, whisk together the olive oil, lemon juice, pepper, and salt.
3. Pour the dressing over the cucumber and tomato mixture and toss to combine.

Nutrition Information:
Serving Size: 1/6 of the salad
Calories: 95
Total Fat: 5 g
Saturated Fat: 1 g
Cholesterol: 0 mg
Sodium: 57 mg
Total Carbohydrates: 11 g
Dietary Fiber: 3 g
Protein: 2 g

11. Mexican Chopped Salad

Mexican Chopped Salad is a flavorful, crunchy, and creamy salad recipe. It is a healthy mix of fresh romaine lettuce, peppers, tomatoes, and jicama with a lime cilantro dressing. This salad can be served as a meal or side dish and is sure to please everyone at your next gathering.
Serving: 4 servings
| Preparation Time: 15 minutes
| Ready Time: 15 minutes

Ingredients:
- 2 cups romaine lettuce, chopped
- 1 red pepper, chopped
- 1 green pepper, chopped
- 1/2 of a jicama, peeled and chopped
- 2 tomatoes, chopped
- 1/2 cup black beans, canned or cooked
- 2 tablespoons fresh cilantro, finely chopped
- 2 tablespoons lime juice

- 2 tablespoons olive oil
- Salt and pepper to taste

Instructions:
1. In a large bowl, combine romaine lettuce, red pepper, green pepper, jicama, tomatoes, and black beans.
2. In a small bowl, whisk together cilantro, lime juice, olive oil, salt and pepper.
3. Pour the dressing over the salad and toss to combine.
4. Serve immediately.

Nutrition Information:
calories: 158, fat: 10 g, carbohydrates: 16 g, protein: 4 g, sodium: 31 mg

12. Pea and Feta Salad

This Pea and Feta Salad is a light and flavorful combination of fresh ingredients. It's easy to make and perfect for a side to just about any meal.
Serving: 4
| Preparation Time: 10 minutes
| Ready Time: 10 minutes

Ingredients:
- 2 cups fresh or frozen peas
- 1/2 cup crumbled feta cheese
- 1/4 cup chopped scallions
- 2 tablespoons olive oil
- 2 tablespoons freshly squeezed lemon juice
- Salt and black pepper

Instructions:
1. Place the peas in a medium bowl.
2. Add the feta cheese, scallions, olive oil, and lemon juice. Stir to combine.
3. Season with salt and pepper.
4. Serve the salad chilled.

Nutrition Information:
- Calories: 219
- Total Fat: 14.1 g
- Saturated Fat: 3.8 g
- Cholesterol: 12 mg
- Sodium: 300 mg
- Carbohydrates: 15.7 g
- Fiber: 4.8 g
- Sugars: 6.2 g
- Protein: 9.1 g

13. Bread and Butter Tomato Salad

Bread and Butter Tomato Salad is a simple, yet delicious tomato salad which combines the flavors of olive oil, salt, pepper, and fresh herbs. Serve with your favorite grilled dish for a light summer meal!
Serving: 4
| Preparation Time: 10 minutes
| Ready Time: 15 minutes

Ingredients:
- 4 tomatoes, diced
- 2 Tbsp butter, melted
- 4 Tbsp olive oil
- 2 tsp salt
- 1 tsp black pepper
- 2 Tbsp fresh herbs (such as basil, chives, oregano), chopped

Instructions:
1. In a medium bowl, combine diced tomatoes, melted butter, olive oil, salt, and black pepper.
2. Stir in fresh herbs and mix until ingredients are thoroughly combined.
3. Scoop mixture into individual serving bowls and allow to sit for 10-15 minutes to allow flavors to come together.
4. Serve with your favorite grilled dish for a light summer meal.

Nutrition Information:
Calories: 110

Fat: 10g
Carbohydrates: 6g
Protein: 1g

14. Mushroom and Asparagus Salad

This savory Mushroom and Asparagus Salad is a delicious and nutritious dish to add to your dinner table. With mushrooms and asparagus as the star of the show, this salad is sure to delight.

Serves 6, | Preparation Time: 10 minutes, | Ready Time: 10 minutes.

Ingredients:
- 3 cups mushrooms, sliced
- 2 cups asparagus, cut into 3-inch pieces
- 2 tablespoons olive oil
- 2 tablespoons balsamic vinegar
- 1 teaspoon mustard
- 1 tablespoon honey
- 1 clove garlic, minced
- Salt and pepper to taste

Instructions:
1. Heat a large skillet over medium-high heat.
2. Add olive oil and mushrooms, and cook for 5 minutes, stirring occasionally.
3. Add asparagus, and cook for 3 minutes more, stirring occasionally.
4. In a small bowl, whisk together balsamic vinegar, mustard, honey, garlic, salt, and pepper.
5. Pour dressing over mushroom and asparagus mixture, and cook, stirring occasionally, until vegetables are tender, about 3 minutes.
6. Serve warm or chilled.

Nutrition Information (per serving):
- 270 calories
- 16 g fat
- 9 g carbohydrates
- 4 g sugar
- 5 g protein

15. Roasted Butternut Squash Salad

This Roasted Butternut Squash Salad is an incredibly satisfying and flavorful dish featuring fresh spinach, feta and currants topped with a creamy, lemon-maple dressing. This dish is vegan friendly, and takes only 35 minutes to prepare.

Serving: 4
| Preparation Time: 10 minutes
| Ready Time: 25 minutes

Ingredients:
-2 lb butternut squash, peeled, seeded and cubed
-2 tablespoons olive oil
-Salt and pepper
-4 cup baby spinach
-1/4 cup feta cheese
-1/4 cup dried currants
- 1/4 cup shelled pumpkin seeds
For the dressing:
-2 tablespoons extra-virgin olive oil
-2 tablespoons maple syrup
-1 tablespoon freshly squeezed lemon juice
- 1/4 teaspoon garlic powder
- Salt and pepper to taste

Instructions:
1. Preheat the oven to 400 degrees F. Place the cubed butternut squash on a baking sheet, and drizzle with the olive oil. Sprinkle with salt and pepper and toss to coat. Roast in the oven for 20 minutes, or until squash is lightly golden.
2. In a large bowl, add the roasted butternut squash, baby spinach, feta, currants and pumpkin seeds.
3. To make the dressing, whisk together the olive oil, maple syrup, lemon juice, garlic powder, salt and pepper in small bowl.
4. Drizzle the dressing over the salad and toss to coat. Serve and enjoy!

Nutrition Information:

Calories: 222; Total Fat: 12g; Saturated Fat: 3g; Cholesterol: 8mg; Sodium: 179mg; Carbohydrates: 25g; Fiber: 4g; Protein: 5g; Sugars: 9g.

16. Red Potato and Dill Salad

This delicious Red Potato and Dill Salad is a perfect side dish at BBQs, potlucks, or weeknight dinners. It's easy to prepare, and its mix of flavors are sure to make it a hit with family and guests alike.
Serving: 4
| Preparation Time: 10 minutes
| Ready Time: 35 minutes

Ingredients:
- 3 pounds red potatoes, quartered
- 2 tablespoons olive oil
- 2 tablespoons dill, chopped
- 1 teaspoon garlic powder
- 2 tablespoons Dijon mustard
- 2 tablespoons red onion, chopped
- 1/4 cup apple cider vinegar
- 2 tablespoons parsley, chopped
- Salt and pepper to taste

Instructions:
1. Preheat the oven to 350F.
2. On a large baking sheet, toss the potatoes with the olive oil, garlic powder and dill.
3. Roast the potatoes for 25-30 minutes, until lightly browned and tender. Remove from the oven and let cool.
4. In a large bowl, combine the potatoes with the onion, mustard, vinegar and parsley. Season to taste with salt and pepper.
5. Serve immediately or chill in the refrigerator until ready to serve.

Nutrition Information:
Per Serving - Calories: 220; Total Fat: 5g; Cholesterol: 0mg; Sodium: 86mg; Total Carbohydrates: 40g; Protein: 5g; Fiber: 5g.

17. Zucchini Ribbon Salad

This delicious Zucchini Ribbon Salad is an easy and flavorful way to enjoy fresh vegetables. Serve it as a side dish or eat it as a light meal.
Serving: 4
| Preparation Time: 10 minutes
| Ready Time: 10 minutes

Ingredients:
- 2 medium zucchinis
- 2 tablespoons olive oil
- Juice from 1 lemon
- 2 tablespoons chopped fresh parsley
- 2 tablespoons chopped fresh mint
- Salt and freshly ground black pepper to taste
- 2 tablespoons crumbled feta cheese

Instructions:
1. Using a vegetable peeler, make thin ribbons from the zucchini.
2. Place the zucchini ribbons in a bowl and toss with the oil and lemon juice.
3. Stir in the parsley and mint.
4. Season with salt and pepper.
5. Sprinkle with feta cheese and serve.

Nutrition Information:
Calories: 152, Fat: 10g, Carbs: 9g, Protein: 5g

18. Roasted Sweet Potato Salad

A simple vegan salad that takes the classic potato salad to a new level, Roasted Sweet Potato Salad is a delicious, nutritious side dish. Perfect for any occasion, this flavor-packed salad is bursting with roasted sweet potatoes, crunchy walnuts, a zesty garlic-lemon vinaigrette, and fresh parsley and basil.
Serving: 4-6
| Preparation Time: 10 minutes
| Ready Time: 35 minutes

Ingredients:
- 3 sweet potatoes (about 2 lbs), cubed
- 2 tablespoons olive oil
- 1/4 teaspoon garlic powder
- 1 teaspoon salt
- 1/4 teaspoon ground black pepper
- 1/4 cup chopped walnuts
- 1/4 cup chopped parsley
- 1/4 cup chopped basil

For the vinaigrette:
- 2 tablespoons olive oil
- 2 tablespoons lemon juice
- 1 garlic clove, minced
- Salt and pepper, to taste

Instructions:
1. Preheat oven to 400F (200°C). Line a baking sheet with parchment paper.
2. Place cubed sweet potatoes on the baking sheet and drizzle with olive oil. Season with garlic powder, salt and pepper, and toss to combine.
3. Roast in preheated oven for 25-30 minutes, or until potatoes are tender and lightly browned.
4. Meanwhile, prepare the vinaigrette by combining all ingredients in a small bowl and whisking until well combined.
5. Transfer roasted potatoes to a large bowl and allow to cool. Add walnuts, parsley, and basil, and pour the vinaigrette over the mixture. Toss to combine.
6. Serve immediately, or cover and chill until ready to serve.

Nutrition Information:
Calories: 166 kcal, Carbohydrates: 24 g, Protein: 3 g, Fat: 8 g, Saturated Fat: 1 g, Sodium: 407 mg, Potassium: 517 mg, Fiber: 3 g, Sugar: 5 g, Vitamin A: 10736 IU, Vitamin C: 14 mg, Calcium: 29 mg, Iron: 1 mg.

19. Grilled Corn Salad

Grilled Corn Salad is a delicious and nutritious dish that can be enjoyed hot or cold, as a side or a main meal. It is made with savory grilled corn and a variety of nutritious, colorful vegetables.

Serving: 8

| Preparation Time: 15 minutes| Ready Time: 25 minutes

Ingredients:
- 4 ears of corn, husks and silks removed
- 1 red bell pepper, seeded and diced
- 1 pint of cherry tomatoes, halved
- 1/4 cup diced red onion
- 2 tablespoons extra-virgin olive oil
- Juice of 1/2 lime
- 1/4 teaspoon garlic powder
- 1/4 teaspoon smoked paprika
- 2 tablespoons chopped fresh cilantro
- 2 tablespoons feta cheese, crumbled (optional)
- Salt and pepper to taste

Instructions
1. Heat an outdoor grill or stovetop grill pan to medium-high heat.
2. Grill the ears of corn, turning every few minutes, until lightly charred and cooked through, about 8 to 10 minutes.
3. Allow the corn to cool before cutting the kernels off the cob.
4. In a large bowl, combine the grilled corn, bell pepper, tomatoes and red onion.
5. In a small bowl, whisk together the olive oil, lime juice, garlic powder and smoked paprika. Pour over the salad and toss everything together.
6. Top with cilantro, feta cheese and season with salt and pepper to taste.
7. Serve.

Nutrition Information:
Serving: 1 cup | Calories: 88kcal | Carbohydrates: 11g | Protein: 2g | Fat: 5g | Saturated Fat: 1g | Sodium: 91mg | Fiber: 2g | Sugar: 4g

20. Roasted Eggplant Salad

Roasted Eggplant Salad is a delicious Mediterranean-style dish, full of flavor and packed with nutrition. Enjoy as a side or main dish, it is sure to be a hit with the family!

Serving: 4
| Preparation Time: 15 minutes
| Ready Time: 45 minutes

Ingredients:
- 2 large eggplants
- 2 garlic cloves, minced
- 3 tablespoons olive oil
- 1 tablespoon balsamic vinegar
- 1 teaspoon dried oregano
- Salt & freshly ground black pepper, to taste
- 2 tablespoons freshly chopped parsley
- 1/2 cup crumbled feta cheese

Instructions:
1. Preheat oven to 425° F.
2. Cut eggplants into 1/2-inch cubes and place in a large bowl.
3. In a small bowl, mix together garlic, olive oil, balsamic vinegar, oregano, salt, and pepper.
4. Pour the olive oil mixture over the eggplant cubes and mix until everything is evenly coated.
5. Spread the eggplant cubes into a single layer on a baking sheet and roast for 40 minutes, stirring occasionally, until the eggplant is tender and lightly browned.
6. Transfer to a serving bowl and add parsley and feta cheese.
7. Serve warm or at room temperature.

Nutrition Information (per serving):
Calories: 197, Fat: 13g, Sodium: 213mg, Carbohydrates: 16g, Fiber: 6g, Protein:6g

21. Roasted Asparagus and Red Onion Salad

Roasted Asparagus and Red Onion Salad is a flavorful side dish that is perfect for any gathering or occasion. The asparagus and red onion are roasted to perfection and mixed with arugula and a simple vinaigrette dressing to really bring out the flavors of the dish.

Serving: 4-6

| Preparation Time: 15 minutes

| Ready Time: 30 minutes

Ingredients:
- 1 lb. fresh asparagus, trimmed
- 1/2 red onion, sliced
- 2 cups fresh arugula
- 1/4 cup olive oil
- 2 tablespoons white wine vinegar
- 1 teaspoon garlic powder
- Salt and pepper to taste

Instructions:
1. Preheat the oven to 400F and lightly grease a baking sheet.
2. Place the asparagus and red onion slices on the baking sheet and drizzle with olive oil.
3. Roast in the oven for 20 minutes, stirring once or twice during the cooking time.
4. In a small bowl, whisk together the white wine vinegar, garlic powder, salt and pepper.
5. Remove the asparagus and red onions from the oven and place in a large bowl.
6. Pour the dressing over the vegetables and toss to combine.
7. Place the arugula on top of the vegetables.
8. Serve the salad warm or cold.

Nutrition Information (per serving):
Calories: 139 kcal, Fat: 10.2g, Carbohydrates: 8.9g, Protein: 4.4g, Fiber: 2.6g, Sugar: 3.5g

22. Cauliflower and Chickpea Salad

This Cauliflower and Chickpea Salad is bursting with bright and vibrant flavors. The combination of crunchy cauliflower, roasted chickpeas, and sweet red onion are a perfect match. The salad is further complemented by a creamy dressing that adds a vibrant burst of flavor.

Serving: 4

| Preparation Time: 10 minutes

| Ready Time: 30 minutes

Ingredients:
- 2 cups freshly chopped cauliflower
- 1 can chickpeas, drained and rinsed
- 1/2 red onion, chopped
- 2 tablespoons olive oil
- 1/4 teaspoon garlic powder
- 2 tablespoons white wine vinegar
- 1/4 cup vegan yogurt
- 2 tablespoons freshly chopped parsley
- Salt and pepper to taste

Instructions:
1. Preheat oven to 350F.
2. On a lined baking sheet, spread out chopped cauliflower and chickpeas. Drizzle olive oil and sprinkle garlic powder over them. Toss everything until evenly coated and spread out in one layer.
3. Roast in the preheated oven for 25-30 minutes, stirring a few times during the roasting process.
4. Meanwhile, in a small bowl, mix together the white wine vinegar and vegan yogurt until combined.
5. Once the cauliflower and chickpeas are finished roasting, allow to cool.
6. When cooled, transfer to a large bowl and add the red onion, parsley, and dressing. Toss everything together until evenly coated.
7. Add salt and pepper to taste.

Nutrition Information:
Calories: 89
Fat: 5.2 g
Carbohydrates : 7.2 g
Protein: 3.8 g

23. Lentil Quinoa Salad

This Lentil Quinoa Salad is a hearty and delicious salad that is perfect for lunch or as a side dish. It features a mix of lentils, quinoa, vegetables and a zesty dressing. It's healthy, wholesome and takes just 25 minutes to cook.

Serving: Serves 4 people
| Preparation Time: 10 minutes
| Ready Time: 25 minutes

Ingredients:
- 1 cup lentils
- 1 cup quinoa
- 2 cups water
- 2 cups diced vegetables (e.g. bell pepper, cucumber, carrots, celery)
- 1 tsp garlic powder
- 2 tsp dried thyme
- 2 tsp ground chilli powder
- 2 tsp dried oregano
- 2 tbsp olive oil
- 1/4 cup apple cider vinegar
- 1/4 cup fresh parsley, finely chopped

Instructions:
1. Rinse lentils and quinoa and add to a medium pot along with water. Bring to a boil then reduce heat to low and simmer for 20 minutes or until lentils and quinoa are cooked.
2. Meanwhile, mix together the diced vegetables and season with garlic powder, thyme, chilli powder, oregano, and olive oil. Set aside.
3. When the lentils and quinoa are cooked, remove from heat and strain any remaining water. Add drained lentils and quinoa to a large bowl along with the seasoned vegetables.
4. Pour the apple cider vinegar over the mixture and stir until evenly combined. Add fresh parsley and toss.

Nutrition Information:
Serving Size: 1/4 of recipe
Calories: 212kcal, Fat: 8.2g, Cholesterol: 0mg, Sodium: 147mg, Carbohydrates: 24.9g, Protein: 9.6g, Fiber: 7.2g

24. Roasted Beet Salad

Roasted Beet Salad is a delicious and vibrant salad made with roasted beets, feta cheese, and spinach, tossed together in a light vinaigrette dressing. This salad is a perfect entrée for any occasion!

Serving: 8-10 servings
| Preparation Time: 15 minutes
| Ready Time: 25 minutes

Ingredients:
- 4 large beets, peeled and cubed
- 4 cups spinach
- 1/4 cup crumbled feta cheese
- 2 tablespoons olive oil
- 2 tablespoons balsamic vinegar
- 2 tablespoons honey
- 1 tablespoon minced garlic
- 1 teaspoon Dijon mustard
- 1/4 teaspoon salt
- 1/4 teaspoon black pepper

Instructions:
1. Preheat oven to 400 degrees F (204 degrees C).
2. Place beets in a single layer on a baking sheet. Drizzle with 1 tablespoon of olive oil and sprinkle with salt.
3. Roast beets in preheated oven for 25 minutes or until tender.
4. In a large bowl, combine the roasted beets, spinach, and feta cheese.
5. In a separate bowl whisk together olive oil, balsamic vinegar, honey, minced garlic, Dijon mustard, salt, and pepper.
6. Pour vinaigrette over the beet salad and combine until all the ingredients are evenly coated.
7. Serve chilled or at room temperature.

Nutrition Information:
Calories: 107kcal | Carbohydrates: 12g | Protein: 3g | Fat: 6g | Saturated Fat: 1g | Cholesterol: 4mg | Sodium: 240mg | Potassium: 360mg | Fiber: 3g | Sugar: 9g | Vitamin A: 824IU | Vitamin C: 6mg | Calcium: 75mg | Iron: 1mg

25. Broccoli and Raisin Salad

This Broccoli and Raisin Salad is a delicious mix of crunchy broccoli, sweet raisins and a tangy dressing - perfect for a side dish or a main meal!
Serving: 4
| Preparation Time: 15 minutes
| Ready Time: 15 minutes

Ingredients:
- 2 cups finely chopped fresh broccoli florets
- 1/2 cup raisins
- 1/4 cup sliced almonds
- 1/4 cup mayonnaise
- 2 tablespoons apple cider vinegar
- 1 tablespoon honey
- 1/4 teaspoon salt

Instructions:
1. In a medium bowl, combine the chopped broccoli, raisins and almonds.
2. In a small bowl, whisk together the mayonnaise, apple cider vinegar, honey, and salt.
3. Pour the dressing over the broccoli mixture and toss to coat evenly.
4. Refrigerate the salad for at least 15 minutes before serving.

Nutrition Information:
Calories: 140, Fat: 8.2g, Protein: 3.1g, Carbs: 15.3g, Fiber: 2.3g, Sodium: 136mg

26. Roasted Sausage and Cabbage Salad

This roasted sausage and cabbage salad is a hearty and delicious meal, brimming with flavorful sausage and crunchy cabbage. This meal is easy to prepare and ready in just over an hour.
Serving: 4
| Preparation Time: 15 minutes

| Ready Time: 1 hour

Ingredients:
- 8 ounces smoked sausage, sliced
- 2 tablespoons olive oil
- 1/4 teaspoon garlic powder
- 1/4 teaspoon paprika
- 6 cups finely chopped cabbage
- 1/2 cup chopped onion
- 2 tablespoons Dijon mustard
- 1 tablespoons white vinegar

Instructions:
1. Preheat your oven to 375 degrees Fahrenheit.
2. Spread the smoked sausage slices onto a baking sheet and drizzle them with olive oil. Sprinkle with garlic powder and paprika.
3. Bake in preheated oven for 15 minutes or until golden and cooked through.
4. Meanwhile, place the chopped cabbage and onions into a large bowl.
5. In a small bowl, whisk together the mustard and vinegar, then pour over the cabbage and onions.
6. Once the sausage is done cooking, add it to the bowl with the cabbage and onions and mix until everything is coated in the mustard mixture.
7. Transfer the mixture to a large shallow baking dish and roast for 30-35 minutes at 375 degrees Fahrenheit, stirring occasionally, until everything is golden and cooked through.

Nutrition Information:
Calories: 236 | Fat: 16.7g | Carbs: 9.3g | Fiber: 3.2g | Protein: 13.7g

27. Farro Salad with Spinach

Farro Salad with Spinach is a flavorful and hearty salad perfect for lunch or dinner, bursting with bold flavors and textures.
Serving: 4-6.
| Preparation Time: 10 minutes.
| Ready Time: 30 minutes.

Ingredients:
* 1 cup farro
* 2 tablespoons olive oil
* 2 cloves garlic, minced
* 4 cups baby spinach
* 2 tablespoons freshly squeezed lemon juice
* 2 tablespoons freshly grated Parmesan cheese
* Salt and freshly ground black pepper, to taste

Instructions:
1. Bring 2 cups of water to a boil in a large saucepan. Add the farro, reduce the heat to low, and cook until tender, about 18 minutes. Drain and set aside.
2. Heat the olive oil in a large skillet over medium heat. Add the garlic and sauté until fragrant, about 1 minute. Add the baby spinach and cook until just wilted, about 3 minutes. Remove from the heat and stir in the farro.
3. Add the lemon juice, Parmesan cheese, and salt and pepper to taste. Stir to combine. Serve warm.

Nutrition Information:
Calories: 160 calories, Fat: 5.1g, Carbohydrates: 20g, Protein: 7.3g, Cholesterol: 4mg, Sodium: 121mg, Fiber: 5g.

28. Cucumber Watermelon Salad

Cool and refreshing, this cucumber watermelon salad is the perfect side dish for any summer barbecue! It's easy to make and comes together quickly for a delicious addition to any meal.
Serving: 4
| Preparation Time: 10 minutes
| Ready Time: 10 minutes

Ingredients:
-2 cups watermelon, cubed
-1 large cucumber, chopped
-1/4 cup red onion, diced
-2 tablespoons fresh cilantro, sliced

-2 tablespoons olive oil
-1 tablespoon balsamic vinegar
-Salt and pepper, to taste

Instructions:
1. In a large bowl, combine cubed watermelon, chopped cucumber, diced red onion, and sliced cilantro.
2. Drizzle olive oil and balsamic vinegar over the salad and season generously with salt and pepper, to taste. Toss to combine.
3. Serve immediately. Enjoy!

Nutrition Information (per serving):
Calories: 88, Total fat: 6 g, Saturated fat: 1 g, Cholesterol: 0 mg, Sodium: 5 mg, Carbohydrates: 8 g, Fiber: 1 g, Protein: 1 g.

29. Roasted Cauliflower Salad

This Roasted Cauliflower Salad is the perfect combination of crunchy, nutty and zingy. An easy to make vegan dish, this flavor packed salad will be a hit at any gathering.
Serving: 4
| Preparation Time: 20 minutes
| Ready Time: 45 minutes

Ingredients:
-1 head cauliflower, cut into florets
-4 cloves garlic, minced
-1/4 cup olive oil
-1 teaspoon sea salt
-2 tablespoons nutritional yeast
-1/4 teaspoon ground black pepper
-2 tablespoons freshly squeezed lemon juice
-2 tablespoons chopped parsley
-1/4 cup pomegranate seeds
-1/4 cup roasted smoked almonds, roughly chopped

Instructions:

1. Preheat the oven to 400 degrees F and line a baking sheet with parchment paper.
2. Place the cauliflower florets on the prepared baking sheet and sprinkle with the garlic, olive oil, sea salt, nutritional yeast, and black pepper.
3. Roast the cauliflower for 25 minutes, stirring halfway through, until golden and crispy.
4. Remove from the oven and let cool for 10 minutes.
5. Place the cooled cauliflower in a large bowl and toss with the lemon juice, parsley, and pomegranate seeds.
6. Serve immediately, topped with the roasted smoked almonds.

Nutrition Information:
Nutrition per serving: Calories: 195; Total Fat: 12g; Saturated Fat: 2g; Cholesterol: 0mg; Sodium: 379mg; Carbohydrates: 18g; Fiber: 4g; Sugar: 8g; Protein: 5g.

30. Avocado Spinach Salad

This Avocado Spinach Salad is a delicious and refreshing salad that makes a perfect light lunch or side dish. It's loaded with healthy ingredients and big flavor.
Serving: 4
| Preparation Time: 10 minutes
| Ready Time: 10 minutes

Ingredients:
- 2 avocados, diced
- 2 cups fresh baby spinach
- 1/4 cup diced red onion
- 1/4 cup sliced cherry tomatoes
- 1/4 cup mandarin oranges
- 1/4 cup crumbled feta cheese
- 1 tablespoon olive oil
- 1/4 teaspoon salt
- 2 teaspoons fresh lemon juice

Instructions:

1. In a large bowl, combine the diced avocados, spinach, red onion, tomatoes, mandarin oranges and feta cheese.
2. Drizzle with olive oil and season with salt.
3. Squeeze in lemon juice over the top and gently toss to combine.

Nutrition Information:
Calories: 168, Fat: 11.6g, Carbohydrates: 14.3g, Protein: 3.7g, Fiber: 5.5g, Sodium: 192mg, Sugar: 4.5g

31. Arugula and Carrot Salad

Arugula and Carrot Salad is a delicious and healthy side dish, perfect for any occasion. It's quick and easy to prepare and comes together in no time.
Serving: 4
| Preparation Time: 15 minutes
| Ready Time: 15 minutes

Ingredients:
-4 cups baby arugula
-1 cup shredded carrots
-1/4 cup extra-virgin olive oil
-2 tablespoons honey
-2 tablespoons fresh lemon juice
-1/2 teaspoon sea salt
-Freshly ground black pepper

Instructions:
1. In a large bowl, combine the arugula, carrots, olive oil, honey, lemon juice, sea salt, and black pepper.
2. Toss all of the ingredients together until they are evenly coated.
3. Serve immediately.

Nutrition Information:
Calories: 171; Total Fat: 15g; Saturated Fat: 2g; Sodium: 148mg; Total Carbohydrates: 9g; Dietary Fiber: 2g; Protein: 2g.

32. Chickpea Salad with Spinach

Chickpea Salad with Spinach is a delicious and nutritious vegan option that's perfect for a quick and wholesome lunch. It's light and flavorful, making it a great way to fuel up and get a boost of essential vitamins and minerals.

Serving: 4, | Preparation Time: 10 minutes, | Ready Time: 10 minutes,

Ingredients:
1. 1 can chickpeas, drained and rinsed;
2. 2 cups spinach, washed and chopped;
3. 1/2 red onion, diced;
4. 1/4 cup red bell pepper, diced;
5. 2 tablespoons olive oil; juice of 1 lemon;
6. 1/4 teaspoon ground cumin; salt and pepper to taste,

Instructions:
1. Combine the chickpeas, spinach, red onion, and red bell pepper in a large bowl.
2. In a smaller bowl, whisk together the olive oil, lemon juice, cumin, salt, and pepper.
3. Pour the dressing over the salad and mix together.
4. Let sit for 10 minutes to allow the flavors to meld.
5. Divide between four plates and enjoy.

Nutrition Information:
Calories: 223 kcal; Carbohydrates: 22.5 g; Protein: 6.3 g; Fat: 11.5 g; Sodium: 155 mg; Sugar: 3.2 g.

33. Avocado Feta Salad

Avocado Feta Salad is a refreshing and flavorful side dish, with bright flavors of lime juice and herbs, combined with creamy avocados and salty feta cheese. This salad is a delicious option for entertaining or a weeknight dinner side dish.

Serving: 4-6
| Preparation Time: 15 minutes
| Ready Time: 15 minutes

Ingredients:
1. 2 avocados, diced
2. 1/2 red onion, chopped
3. 1/2 cup feta cheese, crumbled
4. Juice of 1 lime
5. 2 tablespoons fresh cilantro, chopped
6. 1 tablespoon olive oil
7. Salt and black pepper, to taste

Instructions:
1. In a large bowl, combine all of the ingredients.
2. Mix together until all ingredients are evenly distributed.
3. Taste and adjust seasoning, if needed.
4. Serve immediately.

Nutrition Information:
Per Serving: 143 Calories; 9.1g Total Fat;32.5mg Cholesterol; 134mg Sodium; 11.5g Carbohydrates; 3.5g Fiber; 2.1g Sugar; 3.5g Protein

34. Artichoke and Olive Sala

This colorful Artichoke and Olive Salad is a light and healthy dish perfect for hot summer days. Serve it as a side to grilled meats or fish, or as a light lunch or snack.
Serving: 4-6
| Preparation Time: 10 minutes
| Ready Time: 10 minutes

Ingredients:
- 2 cans (14 ounces each) artichoke hearts, drained and quartered
- 1/2 cup pitted kalamata olives
- 1/2 cup diced red onion
- 1/4 cup minced fresh parsley
- 2 tablespoons red wine vinegar
- 2 tablespoons extra-virgin olive oil
- 1 garlic clove, minced
- 1/4 teaspoon salt

- 1/4 teaspoon freshly ground black pepper

Instructions:
1. In a medium bowl, combine artichokes, olives, onion, and parsley.
2. In a small bowl, whisk together vinegar, oil, garlic, salt, and pepper.
3. Drizzle dressing over the artichoke mixture and toss to coat.
4. Serve immediately or refrigerate until chilled.

Nutrition Information:
Calories: 185, Total Fat: 11 g, Saturated Fat: 2 g, Sodium: 313 mg, Total Carbohydrates: 17 g, Dietary Fiber: 5 g, Protein: 5 g.

35. Roasted Tomato Salad

Roasted Tomato Salad is a simple and delicious dish that is perfect for any occasion. It features roasted tomatoes combined with fresh mixed greens for a burst of flavor and crunch.
Serves 4. | Preparation Time 10 minutes. Ready in 20 minutes.

Ingredients:
- 2 large tomatoes, sliced in half
- 2 tablespoons olive oil
- 1/2 teaspoon dried oregano
- Salt and freshly ground pepper to taste
- 4 cups mixed greens
- 1 tablespoon chopped fresh basil

Instructions:
1. Preheat oven to 400F. Line a baking sheet with aluminum foil.
2. Place tomato halves on the baking sheet and drizzle with oil; sprinkle with oregano, salt, and pepper.
3. Roast in the oven for 15 minutes.
4. Place mixed greens in a large bowl and top with roasted tomatoes. Sprinkle with fresh basil.

Nutrition Information (per serving):
Calories: 73; Total Fat: 5g; Carbohydrates: 6g; Protein: 1g; Sodium: 3mg; Fiber: 1g; Sugar: 3g.

36. Blueberry Watercress Salad

This refreshing and colorful Blueberry Watercress Salad is a delicious and nutritious way to enjoy fresh seasonal fruits and greens. The blueberries give it a sweet and tangy flavor, while the watercress adds a peppery, herbaceous bite. Enjoy this simple yet delightful salad as a side to any meal or a light lunch.

Serving: 4
| Preparation Time: 15 minutes
| Ready Time: 15 minutes

Ingredients:
- 4 cups of watercress leaves
- 2 cups of blueberries
- 2 ounces of feta cheese, crumbled
- 4 tablespoons olive oil
- 2 tablespoons balsamic vinegar
- Salt and pepper, to taste

Instructions:
1. Rinse the watercress and spin in a salad spinner to remove excess water. Place in a medium bowl.
2. Add the blueberries, feta cheese, olive oil, and balsamic vinegar. Toss to combine.
3. Season with salt and pepper to taste.
4. Divide the salad among four plates and serve.

Nutrition Information:
Calories: 121, Total Fat: 9 g, Saturated Fat: 2 g, Trans Fat: 0 g, Cholesterol: 8 mg, Sodium: 69 mg, Total Carbohydrates: 9 g, Dietary Fiber: 2 g, Total Sugars: 6 g, Protein: 3 g.

37. Tomato and Quinoa Salad

This bright, flavorful and nutrient-dense Tomato and Quinoa Salad is perfect for meal prepping during the week or as a side at any gathering.

Serve this hearty salad with grilled protein or fish and your favorite leafy green salad.
Serving: 4-6
| Preparation Time: 10 minutes
| Ready Time: 25 minutes

Ingredients:
- 1 cup quinoa
- 2 cups vegetable or chicken stock
- 1 pint of cherry tomatoes, halved
- 1 cup cucumber, diced
- 1/2 red onion, diced
- 1/3 cup feta cheese
- 1/4 cup chopped parsley
- Juice of 1/2 lemon
- 1/4 cup extra-virgin olive oil
- Salt and pepper, to taste

Instructions:
- Begin by rinsing quinoa in a fine mesh strainer and combine with vegetable or chicken stock in a medium saucepan. Bring to a boil and then reduce to a simmer for 15 minutes.
- Transfer quinoa to a large mixing bowl and let cool for 10 minutes.
- Add cherry tomatoes, cucumber, red onion, feta cheese, parsley, lemon juice, and olive oil to mixing bowl with cooled quinoa. Toss to combine.
- Season with salt and pepper to taste.
- Serve chilled or at room temperature.

Nutrition Information:
Per Serving:
Calories: 250; Total Fat: 15.6g; Cholesterol: 5.3mg; Sodium: 206.9mg; Potassium: 701.6mg; Carbohydrates: 21.3g; Protein: 7.2g; Fiber: 3.2g; Sugar: 2.6g.

38. Kale and Avocado Salad

This Kale and Avocado Salad is a delicious and nutritious salad that's perfect for any meal or potluck. It's filled with loads of vitamins and antioxidants and is a light and refreshing dish.

Serving: 4

| Preparation Time: 10 minutes

| Ready Time: 10 minutes

Ingredients:

- 3 cups of chopped kale
- 1 medium avocado
- 1 tablespoon olive oil
- 1 teaspoon lemon juice
- 1/4 teaspoon salt

Instructions:

1. Chop your kale into small bite-sized pieces and place into a large bowl.
2. Slice the avocado in half. Use a spoon to remove the seed and discard. Scoop the avocado out of the skin and place it into the bowl with the kale.
3. Drizzle the olive oil and lemon juice onto the kale and avocado and season with salt.
4. Mix everything together until everything is evenly distributed.

Nutrition Information:

- Serving Size: 1
- Calories: 160
- Fat: 12g
- Carbohydrates: 11g
- Protein: 4g

39. Spinach, Apple and Walnut Salad

This Spinach, Apple and Walnut Salad is a perfect way to brighten any meal. Tender spinach and sweet apples are complemented by crunchy walnuts and tart vinaigrette for a fresh and flavorful side dish that's sure to please.

Serving: 4

| Preparation Time: 10 minutes

| Ready Time: 10 minutes

Ingredients:
- 6 cups baby spinach
- 2 apples, cored and diced
- 1/4 cup walnuts, roughly chopped
- 1/4 cup olive oil
- 2 tablespoons white wine vinegar
- 1 teaspoon honey
- Salt and pepper, to taste

Instructions:
1. In a large bowl, combine the spinach, apples, and walnuts.
2. In a small bowl, whisk together the olive oil, vinegar, honey, and salt and pepper.
3. Pour the dressing over the salad and toss to coat.

Nutrition Information: per serving:
Calories: 180 kcals
Carbs: 12 g
Protein: 2.5 g
Fat: 14 g
Fiber: 4 g

40. Roasted Sweet Potato and Quinoa Salad

This Roasted Sweet Potato and Quinoa Salad is a mouthwatering dish packed full of flavor and nutrition. It's perfect for all of your vegan, gluten-free, and dairy-free needs. With plenty of protein and fiber, this meal is sure to satisfy your appetite.
Serving: 4-6
| Preparation Time: 10 minutes
| Ready Time: 30 minutes

Ingredients:
- 2 large sweet potatoes, chopped
- 2 cups cooked quinoa
- 2 tablespoons olive oil

- 2 tablespoons lime juice
- 2 tablespoons chopped fresh cilantro
- 1 teaspoon ground cumin
- 1 teaspoon chili powder
- Salt and pepper, to taste

Instructions:
1. Preheat oven to 375 degrees F and line a baking sheet with parchment paper.
2. Place the chopped sweet potatoes onto the baking sheet and lightly coat with olive oil.
3. Roast for 25-30 minutes until tender and slightly golden brown.
4. In a medium-sized bowl, add the cooked quinoa and roasted sweet potatoes.
5. Pour the olive oil, lime juice, and seasonings over the quinoa and stir until combined.
6. Wash and chop the cilantro and add to the bowl, stirring until combined.
7. Serve the salad warm or chilled and enjoy.

Nutrition Information (per serving):
Calories: 255
Fat: 8g
Carbohydrates: 37g
Protein: 7g
Fiber: 6g

41. Zucchini and Sun-Dried Tomato Salad

This light and sweet Zucchini and Sun-Dried Tomato Salad is a great accompaniment to any summer meal. With its bounty of fresh vegetables and tart sun-dried tomatoes, this refreshing salad will please any palate.
Serving: 6
| Preparation Time: 15 minutes
| Ready Time: 15 minutes

Ingredients:
- 2 zucchini, sliced

- 1/2 cup sun-dried tomatoes
- 1/2 cup pitted black olives
- 1/2 cup chopped fresh parsley
- 1/4 cup extra-virgin olive oil
- 2 tablespoons red wine vinegar
- 1/4 teaspoon sea salt
- 1/4 teaspoon freshly ground black pepper

Instructions:
1. Place the zucchini, sun-dried tomatoes, olives, and parsley in a large bowl.
2. In a small bowl, whisk together the olive oil, vinegar, salt, and pepper. Pour the dressing over the vegetables and toss to combine.
3. Serve the salad immediately.

Nutrition Information (per serving):
Calories 134; Fat 11.2 g; Carbohydrates 8.7 g; Protein 2.2 g; Sodium 181 mg; Fiber 2.7 g

42. Cucumber and Radish Salad

This delicious and healthy Cucumber and Radish Salad is bursting with crunch and flavor. This salad is the perfect summer side dish and goes great with any meal.
Serve: 4
| Preparation Time: 5 minutes
| Ready Time: 10 minutes

Ingredients:
-1 cucumber, thinly sliced
-2 Radishes, thinly sliced
-1 teaspoon freshly chopped dill
-1/4 teaspoon of sea salt
-1/4 teaspoon of freshly cracked pepper
-1 tablespoon of freshly squeezed lemon juice

Instructions:
1. Begin by slicing the cucumber and radishes very thinly.

2. Place the cucumber and radishes into a bowl.
3. Add the dill, salt, and pepper and toss everything together until it is evenly mixed.
4. Squeeze the lemon juice over the salad and mix everything together.
5. Serve chilled.

Nutrition Information:
Serving size 4; Per serving: Calories 30; Carbs 6g; Fat 0g; Protein 1g; Sodium 200mg.

43. Broccoli and Red Pepper Salad

Broccoli and Red Pepper Salad is a hearty, colorful dish, packed with nutritious vegetables and flavors. It is ideal as a side dish to a variety of meals, or as a light lunch or snack.
Serving: 6-8
| Preparation Time: 10 minutes
| Ready Time: 10 minutes

Ingredients:
- 2 heads of broccoli, florets only
- 2 cups red peppers, diced
- 2 tablespoons olive oil
- 3 tablespoons white wine vinegar
- 2 tablespoons fresh chopped parsley
- 1 teaspoon sugar
- 1/4 teaspoon garlic powder
- Pinch of salt and pepper

Instructions:
1. In a large bowl, combine the broccoli florets and diced red peppers.
2. In a separate bowl, mix together the olive oil, white wine vinegar, fresh chopped parsley, sugar, garlic powder, salt, and pepper.
3. Pour the dressing over the broccoli and red pepper and mix until all the ingredients are evenly coated. Serve the salad chilled or at room temperature.

Nutrition Information:

Calories: 64 kcal; Carbohydrates: 7 g; Protein: 3 g; Fat: 4 g; Sodium: 57 mg; Potassium: 333 mg; Fiber: 2 g; Sugar: 3 g; Vitamin A: 1414 IU; Vitamin C: 116 mg; Calcium: 24 mg; Iron: 1 mg.

44. Arugula and Almond Salad

Arugula and Almond Salad is a delicious and healthy salad that is full of flavor and crunch. Served best with a light vinaigrette dressing, it makes an excellent side dish or light lunch.
Serving: 4
| Preparation Time: 10 minutes
| Ready Time: 10 minutes

Ingredients:
- 4 cups Arugula
- 2 tablespoons toasted, slivered Almonds
- 2 tablespoons olive oil
- 1 tablespoon white Wine Vinegar
- Salt and Pepper to taste

Instructions:
1. Wash and dry the arugula and set aside.
2. Toast the slivered almonds in a pan over medium heat until lightly browned. Transfer to a plate to cool.
3. In a small bowl combine the olive oil, white wine vinegar, salt, and pepper.
4. In a large bowl, combine the arugula and toasted almonds.
5. Drizzle the vinaigrette over the salad and toss to combine.
6. Serve the salad immediately.

Nutrition Information: (per serving)
- Calories - 135
- Carbohydrates- 2 g
- Protein - 2 g
- Fat - 13 g
- Saturated Fat - 1 g
- Sodium – 30 mg
- Fiber - 1g

45. Red Potato and Green Bean Salad

This Red Potato and Green Bean Salad is a light and flavorful side dish that is simple to make and full of nutritious ingredients. It's perfect for summer barbecues or weeknight dinners.
Serving: 4-6
| Preparation Time: 10 minutes
| Ready Time: 25 minutes

Ingredients:
- 4 cups red potatoes, cut into quarters
- 2 cups green beans, cut into 1-inch pieces
- 2 tablespoons olive oil
- 1/2 teaspoon garlic powder
- 1/2 teaspoon dried oregano
- 2 tablespoons fresh lemon juice
- 2 tablespoons chopped fresh parsley
- Salt and pepper, to taste

Instructions:
1. Bring a large pot of salted water to a boil. Add potatoes and cook for 10 minutes. Add green beans and cook until tender, about 5 minutes more.
2. Drain potatoes and green beans and transfer to a large bowl.
3. Toss potatoes and beans with olive oil, garlic powder, oregano, lemon juice, and parsley. Season to taste with salt and pepper.
4. Serve warm or cold.

Nutrition Information (per serving):
 Calories: 147, Total Fat: 3.7g, Saturated Fat: 0.5g, Cholesterol: 0mg, Sodium: 16mg, Carbohydrates: 26.4g, Fiber: 3.4g, Sugar: 2.3g, Protein: 3.3g.

46. Potato and Parsley Salad

Potato and Parsley Salad is a delicious and nutritious dish that is perfect for lunch or dinner. It combines potatoes and parsley with other flavorful ingredients to make a light, flavorful salad. The dish can be served for 4 people and it takes 30 minutes to prepare and 2 hours to let chill.
Serving: 4
| Preparation Time: 30 minutes
| Ready Time: 2 hours

Ingredients:
- 2 lbs of potatoes, peeled and cubed
- 1/2 cup of fresh parsley, chopped
- 1/4 cup of roasted pine nuts
- 2 tablespoons of red-wine vinegar
- 2 tablespoons of extra-virgin olive oil
- Salt and freshly ground pepper, to taste

Instructions:
1. Bring a large saucepan of salted water to a boil. Add the potatoes and cook until tender, about 10 minutes.
2. Drain the potatoes and transfer them to a large bowl.
3. Let the potatoes cool for about 10 minutes.
4. Add the parsley, pine nuts, red-wine vinegar, and extra-virgin olive oil. Mix until all the ingredients are combined.
5. Season with salt and pepper, to taste.
6. Place the salad in the refrigerator for 2 hours.

Nutritional Information:
Calories: 250 / Total Fat: 11g / Saturated Fat: 2g / Cholesterol: 0mg / Sodium: 20mg / Carbohydrates: 36g / Dietary Fiber: 4g / Protein: 4g

47. Beet and Goat Cheese Salad

Beet and Goat Cheese Salad is a delicious and healthy salad recipe packed with flavor. This salad is a great way to enjoy colorful beets, tangy goat cheese, and peppery arugula. Serve as a main dish or side dish to complete any meal.
Servings: 4

| Preparation Time: 10 minutes
| Ready Time: 15 minutes

Ingredients:
- 4 medium-size beets, peeled, quartered and thinly sliced
- 2 cups arugula
- 1/4 cup of extra-virgin olive oil
- 4 ounces crumbled goat cheese
- 3 tablespoons of balsamic vinegar
- Salt and pepper to taste

Instructions:
1. Preheat oven to 375 degrees.
2. Toss sliced beets with olive oil and place onto a baking sheet.
3. Bake for 15-20 minutes, stirring once or twice, until beets are lightly browned.
4. Remove from oven and set aside.
5. In a large bowl, add arugula, beets, salt, pepper, and balsamic vinegar. Gently toss to combine.
6. Add goat cheese and toss once more.
7. Serve immediately.

Nutrition Information (per serving):
Calories: 214, Fat: 17.5g, Cholesterol: 14mg, Sodium: 187.7mg, Carbohydrates: 8.7g, Protein: 8.7g

48. Carrot and Cabbage Salad

This Carrot and Cabbage Salad is a light and flavorful dish combining carrots and cabbage for a simple yet tasty side. It's perfect for adding to lunch boxes or for rounding off a meal.
Serving: 4-6
| Preparation Time: 10 minutes
| Ready Time: 10 minutes

Ingredients:
- 2 cups shredded carrot
- 2 cups shredded cabbage

- 2 tablespoons extra-virgin olive oil
- 1 teaspoon Dijon mustard
- 1 teaspoon honey
- 1 teaspoon apple cider vinegar
- Salt and pepper, to taste

Instructions:
1. In a large salad bowl, mix together the carrot and cabbage.
2. In a separate bowl, whisk together the olive oil, mustard, honey and vinegar to make a dressing.
3. Pour the dressing over the veggie mixture and season with salt and pepper.
4. Toss ingredients together to evenly distribute the dressing.

Nutrition Information (per serving):
Calories: 70, Total Fat: 4 g, Saturated Fat: 0 g, Total Carbohydrate: 8 g, Protein: 1 g, Sodium: 25 mg, Cholesterol: 0 mg, Fiber: 2 g

49. Roasted Pepper and Onion Salad

This Roasted Pepper and Onion Salad is the perfect side dish for any meal. The sweetness of the roasted peppers, red onion, and tomatoes is balanced by the freshness of the creamy feta cheese and tart lemon vinaigrette.
Serving: 5 - 6 people
| Preparation Time: 10 minutes
| Ready Time: 20 minutes

Ingredients:
- 2 red bell peppers, chopped
- 1 red onion, chopped
- 2 tablespoons olive oil
- 2 tablespoons red wine vinegar
- Salt and pepper
- 2 tomatoes, diced
- 2 tablespoons chopped fresh basil
- 3 ounces feta cheese, crumbled

Instructions:
1. Preheat oven to 350 degrees F.
2. Spread chopped peppers, onions and tomatoes on a baking sheet and lightly coat vegetables with olive oil and season with salt and pepper.
3. Roast vegetables in the preheated oven for 15 to 20 minutes or until vegetables are tender.
4. In a large bowl, combine roasted vegetables with red wine vinegar, basil and feta cheese.
5. Mix gently until all ingredients are evenly combined.
6. Serve warm or chilled.

Nutrition Information:
140 calories, 8 grams of fat, 6 grams of carbohydrates, 6 grams of fiber, 4 grams of protein

50. Lentil and Avocado Salad

Here's an easy and healthy salad filled with protein and minerals the whole family will love. This Lentil and Avocado Salad is the perfect meal for lunch, dinner or a side dish!
Serving: Makes 4-6 servings
| Preparation Time: 15 minutes
| Ready Time: 15 minutes

Ingredients:
- 2 cups cooked and cooled lentils
- 2 avocados, diced
- 1/2 cup feta cheese, crumbled
- 1/3 cup roasted sunflower seeds
- 1/3 cup parsley, minced
- 1 lemon, juiced
- 2 tablespoons extra virgin olive oil
- Salt and pepper, to taste

Instructions:
1. In a large bowl, mix together the lentils, avocado, feta cheese, sunflower seeds and parsley.

2. In a small bowl, whisk together the lemon juice, olive oil, salt and pepper.
3. Pour the lemon salad dressing over the salad and toss to combine.
4. Serve the salad chilled or at room temperature.

Nutrition Information: per serving:
Calories: 307kcal | Carbohydrates: 28.9g | Protein: 13.1g | Fat: 17.7g | Saturated Fat: 3.9g | Cholesterol: 13mg | Sodium: 210mg | Potassium: 724mg | Fiber: 10.8g | Sugar: 1.4g | Vitamin A: 757IU | Vitamin C: 23mg | Calcium: 126mg | Iron: 4mg

51. Greek Quinoa Salad

This Greek Quinoa Salad is a simple yet delicious and healthy Mediterranean-style side dish. It's full of protein thanks to quinoa, vegetables, and feta, and can be served hot or cold.
Serving: 4
| Preparation Time: 15 minutes
| Ready Time: 15 minutes

Ingredients:
- 1 cup quinoa
- 2 cups vegetable broth
- 2 tablespoons olive oil
- 1 cup chopped red bell pepper
- 1 cup halved cherry tomatoes
- 2 cloves garlic, minced
- 2 tablespoons red wine vinegar
- 2 tablespoons freshly squeezed lemon juice
- 1 teaspoon dried oregano
- 1/2 teaspoon salt
- 1/2 cup crumbled feta cheese
- 1/4 cup chopped fresh parsley

Instructions:
1. In a medium saucepan over medium-high heat, bring quinoa and vegetable broth to a boil. Reduce heat to low, cover, and simmer for 15 minutes, or until quinoa is cooked through and liquid is absorbed.

2. Heat olive oil in a large skillet over medium heat. Add bell pepper, tomatoes, and garlic. Cook for 5 minutes, stirring occasionally, until vegetables are tender.
3. In a small bowl, whisk together red wine vinegar, lemon juice, oregano, and salt.
4. In a large bowl, combine cooked quinoa and cooked vegetables. Add vinegar mixture and mix until combined. Gently fold in feta cheese and parsley.

Nutrition Information:
Per serving: 240 calories, 14g fat, 2g saturated fat, 12g carbohydrates, 3g protein, 2g dietary fiber, 300mg sodium.

52. Roasted Cauliflower and Feta Salad

This delicious Roasted Cauliflower and Feta Salad is a great option for a light, flavorful summer meal. It comes together in just 30 minutes of prep and cooking time and serves four. Made with both sweet and savory ingredients like roasted cauliflower, cherry tomatoes, and feta cheese, this salad is an ideal addition to any lunch or dinner.

Serving: 4
| Preparation Time: 10 minutes
Cook Time: 20 minutes
| Ready Time: 30 minutes

Ingredients:
- 6 cups cauliflower florets, cut into 1-inch pieces
- 2 tablespoons olive oil
- 1/2 teaspoon salt
- 1/2 teaspoon black pepper
- 1/2 teaspoon garlic powder
- 1/2 cup crumbled feta cheese
- 1/2 cup halved cherry tomatoes
- 2 tablespoons chopped fresh parsley

Instructions:

1. Preheat oven to 400F. On a large rimmed baking sheet, toss together the cauliflower florets, olive oil, salt, pepper, and garlic powder. Spread into an even layer.
2. Roast for 20 minutes, stirring once halfway through.
3. Transfer to a serving bowl. Add the feta cheese, cherry tomatoes, and parsley, and gently toss everything together.
4. Serve the salad warm or cold.

Nutrition Information:
Serving size: 1/4 of recipe
Calories: 120
Fat: 7g
Saturated fat: 2g
Carbohydrates: 10g
Sugar: 4g
Protein: 4g

53. Roasted Beet and Walnut Salad

Roasted Beet and Walnut Salad is a nutritious and delicious salad perfect for any occasion. This salad brings together the sweet flavor of roasted beets and the crunchy texture of walnuts, along with ripe tomatoes, crumbly feta cheese and a drizzle of balsamic dressing. Topped with fresh parsley, it's a stunning dish that's sure to please.
Serving: 4-6
| Preparation Time: 10 minutes
| Ready Time: 10 minutes

Ingredients:
- 4 large beets
- 4 tablespoons walnuts
- 1 pint cherry tomatoes, halved
- 4 ounces feta cheese
- 2 tablespoons fresh parsley
- 2 tablespoons olive oil
- 1 tablespoon white balsamic vinegar
- Salt and pepper to taste

Instructions:
1. Preheat the oven to 400F.
2. Wrap the beets in aluminum foil. Roast for 45 minutes or until tender when pierced with a fork.
3. Meanwhile, heat a large skillet over medium heat. Add the walnuts and toast for about 2 minutes, stirring often.
4. Allow the beets to cool and then cut each into eight wedges.
5. Place the beets in a large bowl with the tomatoes, feta cheese and parsley.
6. In a small bowl, whisk together the olive oil, balsamic vinegar, salt and pepper. Drizzle the dressing over the salad and toss to coat.
7. Transfer the salad to a serving platter and top with the toasted walnuts.

Nutrition Information:
Serving Size: 1 cup
Calories: 123
Total Fat: 10 g
Saturated Fat: 2 g
Cholesterol: 8 mg
Sodium: 114 mg
Total Carbohydrates: 7 g
Dietary Fiber: 2 g
Sugars: 4 g
Protein: 4 g

54. Orzo and Pea Salad

This vibrant Orzo and Pea Salad is a balanced meal with a mix of crunchy vegetables, protein-rich cheese, and hearty pasta. The zesty lemon dressing adds a zing of flavour and the meal can be put together in less than 30 minutes!
Serving: 4-5
| Preparation Time: 15 minutes
| Ready Time: 15 minutes

Ingredients:
- 250g Orzo pasta

- 1/2 cup frozen peas
- 1/2 red onion, sliced
- 1/2 yellow bell pepper, diced
- 2 tablespoons olive oil
- Juice of one lemon
- Salt and pepper to taste
- 1/2 cup Grated Parmesan cheese

Instructions:
1. Bring a pot of salted water to a boil and add the Orzo. Cook until aldente (around 8 minutes).
2. Meanwhile, in a separate bowl add in the peas, red onion, and yellow bell pepper.
3. When the Orzo is cooked, drain it and rinse it with cold water.
4. Add the Orzo to the pea mixture and stir everything together.
5. Make the dressing by whisking the olive oil with the lemon juice, salt and pepper.
6. Pour the dressing over the salad and top with the Parmesan cheese.
7. Mix everything together, taste and adjust seasoning if necessary.

Nutrition Information:
Per Serving: 459 Calories, 25.2g Fats, 30.1g Carbs, 8.7g Protein.

55. Wheatberry and Orange Salad

This refreshing Wheatberry and Orange Salad is a delicious blend of chewy wheatberries, sweet oranges, and a bright herb dressing. Serve it as a side dish to an entree or make it a meal by adding your favorite protein.
Serving: 4; | Preparation Time: 10 min; | Ready Time: 40 min.

Ingredients:
-2/3 cup uncooked wheatberries
-1/3 cup orange juice
-2 oranges, peeled, segmented and chopped
-1/4 cup chopped fresh parsley
-2 tablespoons of olive oil
-2 tablespoons of white balsamic vinegar
-1 teaspoon Dijon mustard

-1/2 teaspoon honey
-Salt and pepper to taste

Instructions:
1. In a medium saucepan, bring 2 cups water to a boil; add wheatberries and simmer for 30 minutes or until tender.
2. Drain the wheatberries and cool for 10 minutes before transferring to a bowl.
3. Combine orange juice, oranges, parsley, olive oil, balsamic vinegar, Dijon mustard, honey, salt and pepper in a separate bowl, whisk to combine.
4. Pour dressing over wheatberries and toss to combine.
5. Refrigerate for at least 30 minutes before serving.

Nutrition Information (per serving):
Calories: 121kcal, Carbohydrates: 15g, Protein: 3g, Fat: 6g, Saturated Fat: 1g, Sodium: 24mg, Potassium: 189mg, Fiber: 3g, Sugar: 5g, Vitamin A: 388IU, Vitamin C: 27mg, Calcium: 37mg, Iron: 1mg

56. Broccoli and Feta Salad

Broccoli and Feta Salad is a delicious and healthy meal that features fresh broccoli, feta, and toasted almonds in a light vinaigrette. It's a great side dish for a variety of entrees or as a light lunch.
Serving: 4
| Preparation Time: 10 minutes
| Ready Time: 10 minutes

Ingredients:
1. 3 cups fresh broccoli florets
2. 1/4 cup of crumbled feta cheese
3. 2 tablespoons extra-virgin olive oil
4. 2 tablespoons white wine or apple cider vinegar
5. Salt and freshly ground black pepper, to taste
6. 1/4 cup of slivered or sliced almonds, toasted

Instructions:
1. Put the broccoli in a large bowl and set aside.

2. In a small bowl, whisk together the olive oil, vinegar, salt, and pepper to make a vinaigrette.
3. Pour the vinaigrette over the broccoli and toss to coat.
4. Add in the feta cheese and almonds, tossing to combine.
5. Serve the salad immediately.

Nutrition Information:
Calories: 122
Fat: 8.6g
Carbohydrates: 7.2g
Protein: 5.4g
Sodium: 194mg
Fiber: 2.8g

57. Roasted Sweet Potato and Feta Salad

This Roasted Sweet Potato and Feta Salad is a simple side dish that's hearty and flavorful. Perfect for a weeknight dinner or special occasion, this salad combines roasted sweet potatoes and feta cheese with delicious leafy greens and a zesty dressing that can't be beat!
Serving: 4
| Preparation Time: 15 minutes
| Ready Time: 45 minutes

Ingredients:
- 2 sweet potatoes, peeled and cut into 1/2-inch cubes
- 2 tablespoons olive oil
- Salt and pepper to taste
- 2 cups baby spinach
- 1/2 cup feta cheese, crumbled
- 1/4 cup sliced almonds
- 1/4 cup dried cranberries
- For the dressing:
- 2 tablespoons olive oil
- 2 tablespoons honey
- 1 tablespoon orange juice
- 1 tablespoon Dijon mustard
- 1 tablespoon white wine vinegar

- Salt and pepper to taste

Instructions:
1. Preheat oven to 375 degrees F.
2. Toss the sweet potatoes in the olive oil, salt, and pepper and spread evenly on a baking sheet. Bake until fork-tender, stirring once, about 25 minutes.
3. Meanwhile, in a large salad bowl combine spinach, feta, almonds and cranberries.
4. In a small bowl whisk together the ingredients for the dressing.
5. Once the sweet potatoes are cooked adds them to the salad and lightly toss.
6. Drizzle the dressing over the salad and lightly toss again.

Nutrition Information:
Calories: 255; Total Fat: 13g; Saturated Fat: 3g; Cholesterol: 9mg; Sodium: 228mg; Carbohydrates: 28g; Sugars: 8g; Fiber: 4g; Protein: 7g.

58. Spinach and Orange Salad

This spinach and orange salad is a delicious combination of sweet and tart flavors. With the crunch of the spinach and the juicy sweetness of oranges, this salad is sure to please everyone.
Serving: Serves 6
| Preparation Time: 10 minutes
| Ready Time: 10 minutes

Ingredients:
- 6 cups fresh spinach leaves
- 3 oranges, cut into wedges
- 1/4 cup slivered almonds
- 1/4 cup crumbled feta cheese
- 2 tablespoons olive oil
- 1 tablespoon white balsamic vinegar
- 2 teaspoons honey
- 1 teaspoon Dijon mustard
- Pinch of salt

Instructions:
1. In a large bowl, combine spinach, oranges, almonds, and feta cheese.
2. In a small bowl, whisk together olive oil, white balsamic vinegar, honey, Dijon mustard, and salt.
3. Pour dressing over salad and gently toss to coat.
4. Serve chilled.

Nutrition Information:
Per Serving (6 servings): Calories: 189, Total Fat: 12 g, Saturated Fat: 3 g, Cholesterol: 8 mg, Sodium: 149 mg, Carbohydrates: 17 g, Dietary Fiber: 5 g, Sugars: 9 g, Protein: 5 g

59. Edamame and Carrot Salad

Bring a delicious and nutritious meal to your plate in minutes with this flavorful Edamame and Carrot Salad. Featuring edamame, crunchy carrots, and a flavorful dressing, this salad is sure to become a family favorite.
Serving: 10-12
| Preparation Time: 10 minutes
| Ready Time: 15 minutes

Ingredients:
- 2 cups shelled edamame, cooked
- 2 cups shredded carrots
- 1/2 cup diced red onion
- 2 tablespoons olive oil
- 1 tablespoon apple cider vinegar
- 1 teaspoon honey
- 1/2 teaspoon salt
- 1/4 teaspoon pepper

Instructions:
1. In a large bowl, combine the edamame, shredded carrots, and diced red onion.
2. In a small bowl, whisk the olive oil, apple cider vinegar, honey, salt, and pepper together to make a dressing.

3. Pour the dressing over the salad and stir until the salad is evenly coated.
4. Serve immediately or chill in the refrigerator until ready to serve.

Nutrition Information:
Calories: 112 kcal, Carbohydrates: 8 g, Protein: 5 g, Fat: 8 g, Saturated Fat: 1 g, Sodium: 146 mg, Potassium: 173 mg, Fiber: 2 g, Sugar: 4 g, Vitamin A: 33 fold, Vitamin C: 1 mg, Calcium: 34 mg, Iron: 1 mg

60. Pickled Cucumber and Tomato Salad

Pickled cucumber and tomato salad is a simple, fresh and flavorful salad with a hint of tang from the pickled cucumbers. It's a great side to any summer meal.
Serving: 4-6
| Preparation Time: 10 minutes
| Ready Time: 45 minutes

Ingredients:
1. 2 cucumbers, thinly sliced
2. 2 tomatoes, cut into wedges
3. 1/2 sweet onion, thinly sliced
4. 1/2 cup white wine vinegar
5. 1 teaspoon kosher salt
6. 1 teaspoon granulated sugar

Instructions:
1. In a bowl, combine the cucumbers, tomatoes, and onion.
2. In a separate bowl, stir together the vinegar, salt, and sugar until combined. Pour the liquid over the vegetables and stir to combine.
3. Cover the bowl and let it sit in the refrigerator for 30-45 minutes.
4. Before serving, pour the vegetables into a strainer and let them sit for a few minutes to remove any extra liquid.

Nutrition Information:
Calories: 45 kcal; Carbs: 9 g; Protein: 1 g; Fat: 0 g; Saturated Fat: 0 g; Cholesterol: 0 mg; Sodium: 456 mg; Fiber: 1 g; Sugar: 5 g.

61. Quinoa Cranberry Salad

This Quinoa Cranberry Salad is a crunchy and easy-to-make healthy dish featuring antioxidant-rich quinoa and cranberries. It is perfect for a light lunch or side dish with any meal.
Serving: 4-6
| Preparation Time: 15 minutes
| Ready Time: 30 minutes

Ingredients:
- 1 cup cooked quinoa
- 1/2 cup dried cranberries
- 2 stalks celery, diced
- 1/2 red onion, diced
- 3 tablespoons fresh parsley leaves, chopped
- 2 tablespoons olive oil
- 1 tablespoon balsamic vinegar
- 1 teaspoon Dijon mustard
- Salt and freshly ground pepper

Instructions:
1. In a bowl, mix together cooked quinoa, dried cranberries, celery, red onion, and fresh parsley.
2. In a separate bowl, whisk together olive oil, balsamic vinegar, Dijon mustard, salt, and pepper.
3. Drizzle the dressing over the quinoa and mix until all ingredients are evenly coated.
4. Refrigerate for at least 30 minutes to allow the flavors to meld before serving.

Nutrition Information:
- Calories: 196
- Fat: 8.3g
- Carbs: 28.3g
- Protein: 4.3g

62. Roasted Root Vegetable Salad

Roasted Root Vegetable Salad is a crunchy and flavorful side dish or main dish. This dish combines the sweetness of roasted root vegetables with a tangy dressing and is full of texture and flavor.

Serving: 4
Prep Time: 10 minutes
| Ready Time: 25 minutes

Ingredients:
1. 2 medium sweet potatoes, peeled and cut into cubes
2. 2 large carrots, peeled and cut into cubes
3. 1 large parsnip, peeled and cut into cubes
4. 1/4 cup olive oil
5. 1 teaspoon dried oregano
6. 1/2 teaspoon garlic powder
7. 2 tablespoons balsamic vinegar
8. 1/4 cup fresh parsley, chopped
9. Salt and pepper to taste

Instructions:
1. Preheat oven to 375F.
2. Place sweet potatoes, carrots, and parsnips in a large bowl and drizzle with olive oil. Sprinkle with oregano and garlic powder and mix until evenly coated.
3. Transfer vegetables to a baking sheet lined with parchment paper and spread out into an even layer.
4. Bake for 20-25 minutes, or until vegetables are tender and lightly browned.
5. In a separate bowl, whisk together balsamic vinegar, parsley, salt, and pepper.
6. When vegetables are done baking, transfer them to the bowl with the dressing and gently mix until all vegetables are evenly coated.
7. Serve warm or chilled.

Nutrition Information:
Serving size: 1 (193 g)
Calories: 183 kcal
Fat: 9 g
Carbohydrates: 24 g

Protein: 3 g
Fiber: 5 g

63. Kale and Artichoke Salad

This delicious Kale and Artichoke Salad is packed with flavor and super simple to prepare. It's perfect for any occasion or even just a light lunch.
Serving: 4
| Preparation Time: 10 minutes
| Ready Time: 10 minutes

Ingredients:
- 2 bunches of kale, destemmed and chopped
- 1/2 cup of artichoke hearts, chopped
- 2 tablespoons of olive oil
- Juice of one lemon
- 1/2 teaspoon of garlic powder
- Salt and pepper to taste

Instructions:
1. In a large bowl, combine the kale and artichoke hearts.
2. Drizzle with the olive oil and lemon juice, then sprinkle with garlic powder, salt, and pepper.
3. Mix until all ingredients are evenly distributed.
4. Serve.

Nutrition Information:
Per serving: Calories: 75, Total Fat: 5 g, Saturated Fat: 1 g, Cholesterol: 0 mg, Sodium: 146 mg, Carbohydrates: 7 g, Dietary Fiber: 2 g, Sugars: 1 g, Protein: 2 g.

64. Barley and Sun-Dried Tomato Salad

This Barley and Sun-Dried Tomato Salad is a delicious summer side dish, perfect for summer barbecues or a simple weeknight dinner.
Serves 6-8, | Preparation Time: 10 minutes, | Ready Time: 40 minutes.

Ingredients:
- 2 cups cooked barley
- 2/3 cup sun-dried tomatoes, chopped
- 1 stalk celery, chopped
- 1/2 cup crumbled feta cheese
- 2 tablespoons white wine vinegar
- 2 tablespoons olive oil
- Salt and pepper to taste

Instructions:
1. In a large bowl, combine the cooked barley with the sun-dried tomatoes, celery and feta cheese.
2. In a small bowl, whisk together the white wine vinegar and olive oil.
3. Pour the vinaigrette over the barley mixture, season with salt and pepper and toss to combine.
4. Cover and chill in the fridge for at least 30 minutes before serving.

Nutrition Information (per serving):
Calories: 214 kcal, Total Fat: 9.5 g, Saturated Fat: 3.2 g, Sodium: 77 mg, Carbohydrates: 25.4 g, Fiber: 3.4 g, Protein: 5.4 g

65. Roasted Carrot and Parsnip Salad

This Roasted Carrot and Parsnip Salad is a delicious and nutritious side dish that is perfect for adding to a weeknight dinner.
Serving: Serves 4
| Preparation Time: 15 minutes
| Ready Time: 30 minutes

Ingredients:
- 8 carrots, peeled and cut into matchsticks
- 4 parsnips, peeled and cut into matchsticks
- 2 tablespoons olive oil
- 2 tablespoons balsamic vinegar
- 2 teaspoons Dijon mustard
- 2 teaspoons honey
- Salt and pepper to taste

Instructions:
1. Preheat oven to 400 degrees.
2. Spread carrots and parsnips onto a baking sheet.
3. Drizzle olive oil over vegetables.
4. Roast for 20 minutes until vegetables are lightly browned and tender.
5. In a small bowl, whisk together balsamic vinegar, Dijon mustard, honey, salt and pepper.
6. In a large bowl, combine roasted vegetables and vinaigrette.
7. Serve warm or cold.

Nutrition Information (per serving):
Calories: 150
Total Fat: 6g
Saturated Fat: 1g
Trans Fat: 0g
Cholesterol: 0mg
Sodium: 256mg
Total Carbohydrates: 21g
Dietary Fiber: 5g
Sugars: 11g
Protein: 3g

66. Roasted Broccoli and Cherry Tomato Salad

This Roasted Broccoli and Cherry Tomato Salad is an easy to make yet hearty salad that makes an ideal lunch or side dish. It's full of flavor with an irresistible combination of roasted vegetables and tangy tomatoes, all bound together with a refreshing lemon and olive oil dressing.
Serving: 6
| Preparation Time: 10 minutes
| Ready Time: 50 minutes

Ingredients:
- 2 heads broccoli
- 1 tbs olive oil
- 3/4 lb cherry tomatoes
- 2 cloves garlic, minced
- 1/4 tsp salt

- 1/4 tsp black pepper
- zest of 1 lemon
- 2 tbs freshly squeezed lemon juice
- 3 tbs extra-virgin olive oil

Instructions:
1. Preheat oven to 400F.
2. Cut the broccoli heads into small florets, and place them in a large baking dish.
3. Drizzle with the olive oil, and toss to coat evenly.
4. Roast for 20-25 minutes, or until the broccoli is lightly browned and crispy.
5. Meanwhile, add the cherry tomatoes and garlic to a separate baking dish and toss with remaining olive oil, salt, and black pepper.
6. Roast for 20-25 minutes, or until the tomatoes are lightly browned and blistered.
7. Once the vegetables are finished roasting, add the lemon zest, lemon juice, and extra-virgin olive oil to a small bowl and whisk together.
8. Add the roasted broccoli and tomatoes to a large bowl and toss with the lemon dressing.

Nutrition Information:
Calories: 164, Protein: 4.5g, Carbohydrates: 14g, Fiber: 4g, Fat: 11g

67. Grilled Peach Salad

This simple and healthy Grilled Peach Salad is perfect for a light summer meal. The sweetness of the grilled peaches combined with the creamy feta, juicy tomatoes, and assorted greens create a delicious and nutritious entrée.

Serving: 6
| Preparation Time: 10 mins
| Ready Time: 15 mins

Ingredients:
* 2 ripe peaches, pitted and halved
* 2 tablespoons olive oil
* 2 tablespoons honey

* 4 ounces crumbled feta cheese
* 1 pint cherry tomatoes
* 2 cups baby spinach
* 2 cups baby arugula
* 1 tablespoon balsamic vinegar

Instructions:
1. Preheat your grill to a medium heat.
2. Brush the peaches with the olive oil and honey, then place them onto the grill. Grill for 3 – 5 minutes, or until charred and softened.
3. Place the spinach, arugula and tomatoes in a large bowl. Top with grilled peaches and crumbled feta.
4. Drizzle with balsamic vinegar and lightly toss to combine.

Nutrition Information:
Calories: 189; Total Fat: 12 g; Saturated Fat: 4 g; Cholesterol: 18 mg; Sodium: 227 mg; Carbohydrates: 16 g; Protein: 6 g; Fiber: 3 g

68. Quinoa and Black Bean Salad

Quinoa and Black Bean Salad is a nutrient-packed vegetarian salad filled with wholesome ingredients including quinoa and black beans. This salad is high in fiber and protein, and can be served as an entrée or side dish.
Serving: 5
| Preparation Time: 10 minutes
| Ready Time: 20 minutes

Ingredients:
-2 tablespoons olive oil
-2 cloves garlic, minced
-1/2 cup quinoa
-1 cup vegetable broth
-1 (15 ounces) can black beans, rinsed and drained
-1 bell pepper, diced
-1/4 cup chopped fresh cilantro
-1/4 cup lime juice
-Salt and pepper, to taste

Instructions:
1. Heat the olive oil in a medium saucepan over medium heat. Add the garlic and quinoa, and cook until the quinoa lightly browns, about 5 minutes.
2. Add the vegetable broth and bring to a boil. Reduce the heat to low, and simmer until all the liquid is absorbed, about 10 minutes.
3. Transfer the cooked quinoa to a large bowl. Add the beans, bell pepper, cilantro, and lime juice. Stir to combine.
4. Season with salt and pepper to taste.
5. Serve the salad at room temperature, or chill it in the refrigerator before serving.

Nutrition Information:
Per serving: 252 calories, 10.3g fat, 33g carbohydrates, 8.7g fiber, 8.3g protein.

69. Raw Kale Salad

Raw Kale Salad is a wholesome, nutrient-dense, and delicious salad that is easy to make and ready to eat in under 30 minutes. With a mix of nutritious vegetables and an easy dressing, it's perfect for a light lunch or side dish.

Serving: 4
| Preparation Time: 10 minutes
| Ready Time: 20 minutes

Ingredients
- 2 bunches of fresh kale, stemmed and destemmed
- 2 carrots, shredded
- 1 red onion, chopped
- 1/2 cup diced tomatoes
- 1/4 cup oil
- 2 tablespoons red wine vinegar
- 1 teaspoon Dijon mustard
- 1/4 teaspoon sea salt
- 1/8 teaspoon black pepper

Instructions

- In a large bowl, combine kale, carrot, onion, and tomato.
- In a small bowl, whisk together oil, vinegar, mustard, salt, and pepper until well combined.
- Pour dressing over salad and toss to combine.

Nutrition Information
Per serving: 154 calories; 11.4 g fat; 9.7 g carbs; 5.1 g protein.

70. Roasted Squash and Onion Salad

This Roasted Squash & Onion Salad consists of deliciously roasted butternut squash and red onions combined with fresh herbs, tangy feta cheese, and a zesty lemon and olive oil dressing. It's a lovely combination of flavors that can be served as a side dish or even a light entree.
Serving: 4
PreparationTime: 10 minutes
ReadyTime: 30 minutes

Ingredients:
1. 1 large butternut squash (2-2.5lbs), peeled, seeded, and cut into 1-inch cubes
2. 1 red onion, cut into wedges
3. 3 tablespoons of olive oil
4. Salt and pepper
5. 3 tablespoons of chopped fresh herbs, such as oregano, thyme, or dill
6. 4 ounces of feta cheese, crumbled
7. Dressing:
8. 2 tablespoons of olive oil
9. 1 tablespoon of freshly squeezed lemon juice
10. Salt and pepper

Instructions:
1. Preheat the oven to 400F.
2. Place the squash and onion wedges on a large baking sheet. Drizzle with the olive oil and season with salt and pepper. Toss to coat; then spread in a single layer on the baking sheet. Roast for 20-25 minutes,

stirring once or twice during this time, until squash and onions are tender.
3. In a large bowl, combine the roasted squash and onions with the chopped herbs and crumbled feta cheese.
4. In a small bowl, whisk together the dressing ingredients. Pour over the salad mixture and gently toss to combine.

Nutrition Information (Per Serving):
Calories: 195
Protein: 5g
Carbohydrates: 18g
Fat: 13g
Fiber: 4g
Sodium: 483mg

71. Avocado Tomato Salad

This tangy and flavorful Avocado Tomato Salad is a delicious and easy-to-make meal that can be served as a side dish or a light lunch. It contains a combination of fresh ingredients that work harmoniously together, resulting in a delicious salad that comes together quickly.
Serving: 4
| Preparation Time: 10 mins
| Ready Time: 10 mins

Ingredients:
1. 2 large tomatoes, diced
2. 1/2 red onion, diced
3. 1 large avocado, diced
4. 1/2 cup fresh cilantro, chopped
5. 1/4 cup lime juice
6. 1/4 teaspoon salt

Instructions:
1. In a medium bowl, combine the diced tomatoes, onion, avocado and cilantro.
2. In a separate small bowl, whisk together the lime juice and salt.
3. Pour the dressing over the salad ingredients and mix to combine.

4. Serve the salad immediately.

Nutrition Information:
Per serving, this salad provides:
Calories: 85
Fat: 5g
Carbohydrates: 8g
Fiber: 4g
Protein: 2g

72. Green Bean and Potato Salad

This Green Bean and Potato Salad is a hearty and flavorful dish that is sure to satisfy. It is a perfect side dish for an outdoor barbecue or a picnic lunch. It takes just a few minutes to prepare and it is sure to be a hit with family and friends.
Serving: 8
| Preparation Time: 10 minutes
| Ready Time: 4 hours

Ingredients:
- 4 cups of cooked and cooled potatoes, diced
- 2 cups of cooked green beans
- 2/3 cup of mayonnaise
- 3 tablespoons of red wine vinegar
- 1 cup of plain Greek yogurt
- 2 cloves garlic, minced
- 1/4 cup of finely chopped sweet onion
- 2 tablespoons of olive oil
- Salt and pepper to taste

Instructions:
1. In a large bowl, combine the potatoes and green beans together.
2. In a separate bowl, whisk together the mayonnaise, red wine vinegar, Greek yogurt, garlic, onion, and olive oil.
3. Pour the dressing over the potato and green bean mixture, and toss to combine.

4. Cover and refrigerate the salad for at least 4 hours before serving, to allow the flavors to blend.
5. Serve the salad with a sprinkle of salt and pepper.

Nutrition Information:
Calories: 134 kcal; Carbohydrates: 14 g; Protein: 3 g; Fat: 8 g; Saturated Fat: 1.5 g; Cholesterol: 5 mg; Sodium: 65 mg; Potassium: 488 mg; Fiber: 2.5 g; Sugar: 0.8 g; Vitamin A: 241 IU; Vitamin C: 17 mg; Calcium: 36 mg; Iron: 2 mg.

73. Roasted Radish and Fennel Salad

This roasted radish and fennel salad is a bright and flavorful dish ideal for any occasion. With simple ingredients and a minimal prep time, this salad is a savory and healthy option for all.
Serve: 4 Servings, | Preparation Time: 5 minutes, | Ready Time: 15 minutes.

Ingredients:
- 16 ounces radishes, halved
- 4 fennel bulbs, thinly sliced
- 2 tablespoons olive oil
- 3 tablespoons lemon juice
- 2 tablespoons freshly chopped dill
- 1 tablespoon salt
- 1/4 teaspoon freshly ground black pepper

Instructions:
1. Preheat oven to 400F.
2. Spread radishes and fennel on a baking sheet and drizzle with olive oil. Roast for 12 to 15 minutes, until vegetables are lightly browned.
3. Transfer roasted vegetables to a bowl and add lemon juice, dill, salt, and pepper. Stir to combine.
4. Serve the salad at room temperature. Enjoy!

Nutrition Information (per serve):
Calories – 123
Carbohydrates – 11.8g

Fat – 7.1g
Protein – 2.7g
Fiber – 4.3g
Sugar – 4.3g

74. Tomato Feta Salad

This delicious Tomato Feta Salad is the perfect summer side dish. Refreshing, light and full of flavor, it combines the sweetness of tomatoes with the salty tang of feta cheese for a flavorful balance. Serve alongside grilled meats or enjoy it on its own as a light meal.
Serving: 4-6
| Preparation Time: 10 mins
| Ready Time: 10 mins

Ingredients:
- 2 & 1/2 cups of halved cherry tomatoes
- 2 cloves garlic, minced
- 3 tablespoons olive oil
- 2 tablespoons balsamic vinegar
- Salt and freshly ground black pepper, to taste
- 2 tablespoons chopped fresh basil leaves
- 2 tablespoons chopped fresh parsley
-1/3 cup crumbled Feta cheese

Instructions:
1. In a large bowl, combine tomatoes, garlic, olive oil, balsamic vinegar, salt and pepper.
2. Add the basil and the parsley and gently combine.
3. Add the feta cheese and gently stir.
4. Serve and enjoy!

Nutrition Information:
Calories: 158; Total Fat: 11.7 g; Sodium: 228 mg; Carbohydrate: 6.9 g; Protein: 6.1 g

75. Radicchio and Red Onion Salad

This simple Radicchio and Red Onion Salad is a light and flavorful side dish that packs a punch of flavor. Perfect for a summer BBQ, this salad comes together in no time and can be served as a side or in a main meal.
Serving: 4
| Preparation Time: 10 minutes
| Ready Time: 10 minutes

Ingredients:
-1 head radicchio, roughly chopped
-2 red onions, thinly sliced into rings
-1/3 cup olive oil
-3 tablespoons balsamic vinegar
-1 teaspoon Dijon mustard
-1 tablespoon sugar
-1 teaspoon fresh thyme, roughly chopped
-2 tablespoons fresh parsley, roughly chopped
-Salt and pepper to taste

Instructions:
1. In a large bowl, combine the radicchio and red onions.
2. In a small bowl, whisk together the olive oil, balsamic vinegar, Dijon mustard, sugar, and fresh thyme.
3. Pour the dressing over the salad and toss to coat.
4. Sprinkle with fresh parsley, salt, and pepper and toss one more time.

Nutrition Information:
Per Serving: 201 Calories; 15g Fat; 1g Protein; 14g Carbohydrates; 4g Dietary Fiber; 8mg Sodium.

76. Greek Chickpea Salad

Greek Chickpea Salad is a light and refreshing salad with juicy tomatoes, crisp cucumber, succulent olives, and tangy feta cheese in a flavorful garlic dressing. It is a great side dish for any summer BBQ or picnic.
Serving: 6
| Preparation Time: 10 minutes

| Ready Time: 10 minutes

Ingredients:
- 1 15.5 oz. can chickpeas, drained and rinsed
- 1 medium cucumber, diced
- 1 pint cherry tomatoes, halved
- 1/4 cup pitted kalamata olives, halved
- 1/4 cup crumbled feta cheese
- 3 tablespoons olive oil
- 2 tablespoons red wine vinegar
- 2 cloves garlic, minced
- 1 teaspoon dried oregano
- Salt and pepper to taste

Instructions:
1. In a large bowl, combine the chickpeas, cucumber, tomatoes, olives, and feta cheese.
2. In a small bowl, whisk together the olive oil, red wine vinegar, garlic, oregano, salt, and pepper.
3. Pour the dressing over the salad and gently toss to combine.
4. Serve chilled or at room temperature.

Nutrition Information (per serving):
Calories: 145, total fat: 12g, cholesterol: 5mg, sodium: 166mg, carbohydrates: 8g, fiber: 3g, protein: 3g.

77. Lentil and Spinach Salad

Lentil and Spinach Salad is a light and flavorful dish that is easy to make and packed with protein and fiber. This simple salad can be served warm or cold, making it a versatile addition to any meal.

Serving 4, this dish takes 15 minutes to prepare and is ready in 30 minutes.

Ingredients:
- 1 cup of dried brown lentils
- 1 bay leaf
- 1 teaspoon of ground turmeric

- 2 tablespoons of olive oil
- 1 onion, diced
- 2 cloves of garlic, minced
- 2 teaspoons of cumin
- 2 cups of spinach leaves
- Salt and pepper, to taste

Instructions:
1. Rinse the lentils and put them in a pot with 2 cups of cold water, the bay leaf, and turmeric on medium heat. Simmer for 15 minutes until the lentils are cooked.
2. Meanwhile, in a large skillet, heat the olive oil over medium-high heat. Add the onion and garlic and cook until softened and golden, about 5 minutes. Add the cumin and cook for another 30 seconds.
3. Once the lentils are cooked, add them to the skillet and mix everything together until combined. Stir in the spinach leaves and cook until wilted, about 2 minutes. Season with salt and pepper to taste.
4. Serve the salad warm or cold.

Nutrition Information:
Serving Size: 1 cup
Calories: 250
Total Fat: 4.5g
Sat Fat: 0.8g
Cholesterol: 0mg
Sodium: 256mg
Total Carbohydrate: 44g
Fiber: 17g
Sugar: 3g
Protein: 10g

78. Broccoli and Sun-Dried Tomato Salad

This Broccoli and Sun-Dried Tomato Salad is bursting with flavor and texture. With sun-dried tomatoes, crunchy broccoli, tart cranberries, and feta cheese, it makes a great side dish.
Serving: 4
| Preparation Time: 10 minutes

| Ready Time: 10 minutes

Ingredients:
* 2 heads broccoli, cut into bite-sized florets
* 1/2 cup chopped sun-dried tomatoes
* 1/4 cup chopped dried cranberries
* 1/4 cup crumbled feta cheese
* 1/4 cup toasted pumpkin seeds
* 1/4 cup extra virgin olive oil
* 2 tablespoons red wine vinegar
* Salt and pepper to taste

Instructions:
1. In a large bowl, combine the broccoli, sun-dried tomatoes, cranberries, feta, and pumpkin seeds.
2. In a small bowl, whisk together the olive oil and red wine vinegar. Pour over the salad and toss to coat.
3. Season with salt and pepper to taste. Serve immediately.

Nutrition Information per serving:
Calories: 151 Fat: 12g Cholesterol: 8mg Sodium: 93mg Carbohydrates: 8g Protein: 3g

79. Lentil, Artichoke, and Feta Salad

This light and fresh Lentil, Artichoke, and Feta Salad is the perfect way to brighten up your lunch or dinner. Served chilled or at room temperature, this salad is full of flavor and texture and is sure to be a crowd-pleaser.
Serving: 6
| Preparation Time: 20 minutes
| Ready Time: 25-30 minutes

Ingredients:
-1 cup uncooked lentils
-2 cups vegetable broth
-1/4 cup chopped red onion
-1/4 cup extra-virgin olive oil

-3 tablespoons fresh lemon juice
-1 teaspoon fresh thyme
-1/2 teaspoon salt
-1/4 teaspoon freshly ground black pepper
-2 cups quartered artichoke hearts
-1/2 cup crumbled feta cheese

Instructions:
1. In a medium saucepan, combine the lentils and vegetable broth. Bring to a boil over high heat, then reduce heat to low and simmer. Cook until the lentils are tender, about 15 minutes.
2. Meanwhile, in a large bowl, combine the onion, olive oil, lemon juice, thyme, salt, and pepper.
3. Add the cooked lentils, artichoke hearts, and feta cheese to the dressing and mix until everything is well combined.
4. Serve chilled or at room temperature.

Nutrition Information:
Calories: 205 | Fat: 10 g | Carbohydrates: 21 g | Protein: 9 g | Sodium: 533 mg | Fiber: 7 g

80. Roasted Chickpea Salad

This Roasted Chickpea Salad is vibrant and flavorful for a delicious plant-based meal. It's packed with roasted chickpeas, kale, crunchy vegetables, and a vibrant tahini dressing. This salad is easy to make and ready in 35 minutes.
Serving: 4 servings
| Preparation Time: 15 minutes
| Ready Time: 35 minutes

Ingredients:
- 2 cans (15 ounces each) chickpeas, drained and rinsed
- 2 cloves garlic, minced
- 2 tablespoons olive oil
- 2 tablespoons old-fashioned oats
- 2 tablespoons nutritional yeast
- Salt and pepper, to taste

- 2 tablespoons tahini
- 1 lemon, juiced
- 2 to 3 tablespoons water
- 2 large bunches kale, stripped and chopped
- 1 large red bell pepper, diced
- 4 small persian cucumbers, diced
- 1 large red onion, diced

Instructions:
1. Preheat oven to 375F.
2. Place the drained chickpeas on a large baking sheet. Add garlic, olive oil, oats, nutritional yeast, salt, and pepper. Toss to combine. Roast for 20-25 minutes until lightly golden and crunchy.
3. Meanwhile, in a small bowl, whisk together tahini, lemon juice, and water. Adjust seasoning with salt and pepper if desired.
4. In a large bowl, combine kale, bell pepper, cucumbers, and onion.
5. When the chickpeas are done roasting, add them to the bowl of vegetables.
6. Drizzle tahini dressing over all and toss to combine.
7. Serve immediately and enjoy.

Nutrition Information (per serving):
195 calories, 8g fat, 19g carbohydrate, 5g fiber, 12g protein

81. Farro and Arugula Salad

Farro and Arugula Salad is an easy, delicious, and healthy meal which is perfect for lunch or dinner. It combines the heartiness of farro, a type of whole grain, with the peppery bite of arugula and the bright pop of a lemony vinaigrette. Serve it as a side dish or pair it with your favorite protein for a complete meal.
Serving: Makes 6 servings
| Preparation Time: 10 minutes
| Ready Time: 10 minutes

Ingredients:
- 1 cup farro
- 2 1/2 cups vegetable broth

- 2 tablespoons olive oil
- 1/2 teaspoon kosher salt
- 5 ounces arugula
- 1/2 cup fresh herbs such as parsley, mint and/or basil, finely chopped
- 1/3 cup walnuts, toasted and finely chopped
- 1 lemon, zest and juice
- 1 tablespoon honey or agave nectar
- 2 tablespoons champagne vinegar
- Freshly ground black pepper

Instructions:
1. In a medium saucepan, bring the farro, vegetable broth, olive oil, and salt to a boil. Reduce the heat and simmer until the farro is tender and the liquid is absorbed, about 25 minutes.
2. In a large bowl, mix together the cooked farro, arugula, herbs, and walnuts.
3. To make the dressing, whisk together the lemon zest and juice, honey, vinegar, pepper and a pinch of salt.
4. Toss the farro and arugula salad with the dressing. Serve.

Nutrition Information:
Per Serving: 274 calories, 16g fat, 28g carbohydrates, 6.7g protein.

82. Cucumber and Tomato Salad with Feta

Cucumber and Tomato Salad with Feta is a light and refreshing side dish, perfect to accompany any summer meal. This delicious combination of crunchy cucumbers, sweet tomatoes, and salty feta cheese is a classic Greek dish and always a crowd pleaser.
Serving: 8
Prep Time: 10 minutes
| Ready Time: 10 minutes

Ingredients:
-3 large cucumbers, cut into thin slices
-2 cups cherry tomatoes, halved
-1/2 cup feta cheese crumbles
-1/4 cup olive oil

-2 tablespoons white wine vinegar
-1 teaspoon minced garlic
-Salt and pepper, to taste

Instructions:
1. In a large bowl, combine the cucumbers, tomatoes, and feta cheese.
2. In a small bowl, whisk together the olive oil, vinegar, garlic, salt, and pepper to make the dressing.
3. Pour the dressing over the cucumbers and tomatoes, and gently toss to combine. Serve immediately.

Nutrition Information:
Serving size: 1/8th of recipe, Calories: 150, Total Fat: 10g, Saturated Fat: 3g, Cholesterol: 15mg, Sodium: 200mg, Total Carbohydrate: 8g, Dietary Fiber: 2g, Total Sugars: 4g, Protein: 4g.

83. Spicy Bean Salad

This zesty salad is bursting with flavor and texture! Spicy Bean Salad is a tasty combination of black beans, corn, peppers, and jalapenos tossed in a spicy and sweet vinaigrette and topped with fresh cilantro and feta cheese.
Serving: 4
| Preparation Time: 10 minutes
| Ready Time: 20 minutes

Ingredients:
- 1 can black beans (15.5 oz), drained and rinsed
- 1 cup sweet corn kernels, cooked
- 1 red bell pepper, seeded and diced
- 1 jalapeno, seeded and diced
- 1/2 cup feta cheese, crumbled
- 1/4 cup fresh cilantro, chopped
- 2 tablespoons olive oil
- 2 tablespoons white wine vinegar
- 1 teaspoon honey
- Salt and pepper to taste

Instructions:
1. In a large bowl, combine black beans, corn, bell pepper and jalapeno.
2. In a small bowl, whisk together olive oil, white wine vinegar, honey, salt and pepper until fully combined.
3. Drizzle the dressing over the vegetables and mix until combined.
4. Sprinkle feta cheese and cilantro over the top of the salad.

Nutrition Information:
per serving: 307 calories, 15.3g fat, 34.5g carbohydrates, 8.2g protein.

84. Quinoa, Avocado and Corn Salad

This flavorful Quinoa, Avocado and Corn Salad is a delicious and nutritious dish, perfect for a light summer meal or side dish. It combines quinoa, avocado, and corn for a wonderfully healthy mix of colors and textures. This salad is ready in a total time of 30 minutes, making it a great choice for a quick and easy dinner.
Serving: 4-6
| Preparation Time: 10 minutes
| Ready Time: 20 minutes

Ingredients:
1. 2 cups cooked quinoa
2. 1 ripe avocado, cut into cubes
3. 1/3 cup sweet canned corn, drained
4. 1/4 cup red onion, diced
5. 1/4 cup crumbled feta cheese
6. 2 tablespoons olive oil
7. Juice of one lemon
8. 2 tablespoons chopped fresh parsley
9. Salt and pepper, to taste

Instructions:
1. In a large bowl, combine the cooked quinoa, avocado cubes, corn, red onion, and feta cheese.
2. In a small bowl, whisk together the olive oil and lemon juice.
3. Pour the olive oil and lemon juice mixture over the quinoa mixture and mix to combine.

4. Stir in the chopped parsley, salt, and pepper.
5. Serve chilled or at room temperature.

Nutrition Information:
Per serving (1/6 of total):
Calories: 212
Fat: 11.9 g
Carbohydrates: 19.8 g
Protein: 6.2 g

85. Kale and Edamame Salad

Kale and Edamame Salad is a delicious, nutritious and healthy side salad that is packed with fresh ingredients and bold flavors.
Serving: 4-6
| Preparation Time: 15 minutes
| Ready Time: 15 minutes

Ingredients:
- 4 cups kale, washed and chopped
- 2 cups cooked edamame
- 1/2 cup feta cheese
- 2 tablespoons olive oil
- 1/4 cup sesame seeds
- 1/2 teaspoon salt
- 1 tablespoon freshly squeezed lemon juice

Instructions:
1. In a large bowl, combine the kale, edamame, feta cheese, olive oil and sesame seeds.
2. Gently toss to combine.
3. Season to taste with salt and lemon juice.
4. Serve immediately.

Nutrition Information:
Calories: 164 kcal, Protein: 8.8 g, Total fat: 10.3 g, Cholesterol: 10 mg, Sodium: 402 mg, Carbohydrates: 10.2 g, Fiber: 3.2 g, Sugars: 1.2 g.

86. Asparagus and Pancetta Salad

This Asparagus and Pancetta Salad is a simple, delicious and healthy side dish that is perfect for entertaining guests. It's full of flavor, texture and color, and can be prepared in under half an hour.
Serving: 6
| Preparation Time: 10 minutes
| Ready Time: 25 minutes

Ingredients:
- 6 ounces pancetta, cut into small cubes
- 1 pound asparagus spears, trimmed and chopped into 1-inch pieces
- 2 tablespoons olive oil
- Juice of 1/2 lemon
- 2 tablespoons Dijon mustard
- 2 tablespoons minced fresh tarragon
- 2 tablespoons minced fresh chives
- 2 tablespoons minced fresh parsley
- 2 tablespoons minced fresh oregano
- Salt and freshly cracked black pepper, to taste

Instructions:
1. In a large skillet over medium heat, fry the pancetta until crisp. Transfer to a paper towel-lined plate.
2 To the same pan, add the asparagus and cook for 3 minutes.
3. In a small bowl whisk together the oil, lemon juice, mustard and herbs.
4. Arrange the asparagus and pancetta onto plates, and drizzle with the dressing.
5. Season with salt and pepper and serve.

Nutrition Information:
81.2 calories, 5.9g fat, 1.7g carbohydrates, 4.6g protein

87. Quinoa, Kale, and Apple Salad

This Quinoa, Kale, and Apple Salad is a hearty combination of textures and flavors! It provides a great balance of protein, fiber, and healthy fats

- plus a delicious dose of antioxidants. The added apples give it a hint of sweetness.
Serving: 8
| Preparation Time: 10 minutes
| Ready Time: 25 minutes

Ingredients:
- 1 cup quinoa
- 1 cup kale, chopped
- 1/4 cup slivered almonds
- 2 apples, chopped
- 1/4 cup olive oil
- 2 tablespoons fresh lemon juice
- 2 teaspoons lemon zest
- 2 tablespoons honey
- Salt and pepper, to taste

Instructions:
1. Cook quinoa according to package instructions.
2. Meanwhile, in a large bowl, combine kale, almonds and apples.
3. In a small bowl, whisk together olive oil, lemon juice, lemon zest, honey, salt and pepper.
4. Once quinoa is cooked, add to bowl with kale.
5. Drizzle dressing over quinoa and kale and toss to combine.
6. Serve chilled or at room temperature.

Nutrition Information:
Per Serving: 230 calories; 11g fat; 27g carbohydrates; 4g protein; 4g fiber; 40mg sodium

88. Sweet Potato and Black Bean Salad

Sweet Potato and Black Bean Salad is a delicious and wholesome meal, perfect for lunch or dinner. This easy to make salad is full of flavorful ingredients and sure to please even the pickiest of eaters!
Serving: 4-6
| Preparation Time: 25 minutes
| Ready Time: 25 minutes

Ingredients:
1. 3 sweet potatoes, diced
2. 1 can black beans, rinsed and drained
3. 1 red bell pepper, diced
4. 2 tablespoons olive oil
5. 2 tablespoons lime juice
6. 1 clove garlic, minced
7. 1 teaspoon ground cumin
8. 1/2 teaspoon chili powder
9. Salt and freshly ground pepper, to taste
10. 1/2 cup diced green onions
11. 1/4 cup chopped cilantro

Instructions:
1. Preheat oven to 400 degrees F. Place the diced sweet potatoes on a foil-lined baking sheet. Drizzle the potatoes with 1 tablespoon of the olive oil and season with salt and pepper. Roast for 20 minutes, flipping once during cooking.
2. In a bowl, combine the black beans, red bell pepper, garlic, cumin, chili powder and the remaining tablespoon olive oil. Toss to combine.
3. In a small bowl, whisk together the lime juice and salt and pepper, to taste.
4. In a large bowl, combine the roasted sweet potatoes, black bean mixture and green onions; pour in the lime juice and toss to combine.
5. Serve the salad topped with chopped cilantro.

Nutrition Information:
Calories: 240, Protein: 7g, Fat: 7g, Carbohydrates: 38g, Fiber: 10g, Sugar: 5g, Sodium: 145mg

89. Roasted Mushroom Salad

This Roasted Mushroom Salad is a nutritious meal of roasted mushrooms and various greens that can be served as either a side dish or as the main course. It is quick to prepare and can be served as soon as it is roasted. The following ingredients provide a flavorful and healthy addition to any meal.

Serving: 4
| Preparation Time: 10 min
| Ready Time: 15 min

Ingredients:
1. 1 lb mushrooms, cut into quarters
2. 2 tbsp olive oil
3. 2 garlic cloves, minced
4. Salt and freshly ground pepper, to taste
5. 1 bag arugula
6. 1/2 cup feta cheese, crumbled
7. 1/3 cup toasted walnuts

Instructions:
1. Preheat the oven to 425F. Place mushrooms on a rimmed baking sheet.
2. In a small bowl mix together the olive oil and garlic cloves. Drizzle over the mushrooms and season with salt and pepper. Roast in the oven for 10 minutes.
3. Remove the mushrooms from the oven and place in a large bowl. Add the arugula, feta and walnuts and gently toss to combine.

Nutrition Information:
Per Serving:Calories 213, Total Fat 15g, Saturated Fat 4g, Trans Fat 0g, Cholesterol 11.9mg, Sodium 250.2mg, Carbohydrates 10.1g, Fiber 2.6g, Sugar 2.8g, Protein 11g

90. Carrot Orange Salad

This Carrot Orange Salad is a delicious combination of sweet carrots, crisp oranges, crunchy walnuts and a light and zesty dressing. A wonderful side dish or light meal, it's quick to make and always hits the spot.
Serving: 4
| Preparation Time: 15 minutes
| Ready Time: 15 minutes

Ingredients:

- 2 cups grated carrots
- 2 oranges, peeled, sliced and quartered
- 1/4 cup walnuts
- 2 Tbsp. olive oil
- 1 Tbsp. honey
- 2 tsp. white vinegar
- 1/4 tsp. ground ginger
- Salt and pepper, to taste

Instructions:
1. In a medium bowl, combine carrots, oranges, and walnuts.
2. In a separate bowl, whisk together olive oil, honey, white vinegar, ginger, and salt and pepper.
3. Pour the dressing over the carrot mixture and stir to combine.
4. Serve chilled or at room temperature.

Nutrition Information: per serving:
Calories: 149, Total Fat: 10g, Saturated Fat: 1.2g, Cholesterol: 0mg, Sodium: 103mg, Total Carbohydrates: 14g, Dietary Fiber: 3.3g, Sugars: 8g, Protein: 2.6g.

91. Grilled Zucchini Salad

Grilled Zucchini Salad combines the delicious flavors of slightly charred zucchini and sweet, juicy tomatoes with herbs, crunchy pine nuts and a tangy balsamic vinaigrette. Perfect for a warm summer dinner.
Serving: 4-6
| Preparation Time: 10 minutes
| Ready Time: 25 minutes

Ingredients:
- 2 medium zucchinis, sliced into 1/4 inch thick rounds
- 1 pint cherry tomatoes, sliced in half
- 2 cloves of garlic, minced
- 2 tablespoons olive oil
- 2 tablespoons basil, chopped
- 2 tablespoons parsley, chopped
- 2 tablespoons pine nuts

- 2 tablespoons balsamic vinegar
- Salt and pepper, to taste

Instructions:
1. Preheat the grill to medium heat.
2. Brush zucchinis with olive oil and season with salt and pepper.
3. Grill zucchini rounds for 5-7 minutes, flipping once, until they have light char marks.
4. Place the grilled zucchini and tomatoes in a large bowl and add in the garlic, basil, parsley, and pine nuts.
5. In a small bowl, whisk together the balsamic vinegar and olive oil.
6. Pour the dressing over the salad ingredients and toss to combine.
7. Serve the salad warm or at room temperature.

Nutrition Information:
Per serving - Calories: 236, Total Fat: 18.4g, Saturated Fat: 2.8g, Cholesterol: 0mg, Sodium: 53mg, Carbohydrates: 16.4g, Fiber: 4.1g, Sugar: 9.6g, Protein: 4.4g.

92. Spinach and Apple Salad

This easy and healthy Spinach and Apple Salad is the perfect side dish to any meal or light lunch. With spinach, apples, walnuts, onions, and a light dressing, its fresh yet comforting flavors come together to create a flavorful and nutritious dish.

Serving: 4-6 | | Preparation Time: 10 minutes | | Ready Time: 10 minutes

Ingredients:
- 5 ounces baby spinach
- 2 red apples, cored and diced
- 1/4 cup walnuts, chopped
- 2 tablespoons red onion, thinly sliced
- 2-3 tablespoons olive oil
- 1 tablespoon apple cider vinegar
- salt and pepper, to taste

Instructions:

1. In a large bowl, combine the spinach, apples, walnuts and red onion.
2. In a separate bowl, whisk together the olive oil, apple cider vinegar, salt and pepper.
3. Pour the dressing over the spinach and toss to combine.

Nutrition Information:
Calories: 135, Total Fat: 8.4g, Cholesterol: 0.0mg, Sodium: 68.7mg, Total Carbohydrate: 14.2g, Fiber: 3.2g, Protein: 2.6g.

93. Roasted Beet, Carrot, and Feta Salad

Roasted beet, carrot, and feta salad with a simple lemon dressing is a delicious and easy side dish that makes a great accompaniment to just about any main course. Its flavor combination of sweet, savory, and tangy make it a crowd pleaser.
Serving: 4
| Preparation Time: 15 minutes
| Ready Time: 25 minutes

Ingredients:
- 5 small beets, scrubbed and cut into 1/4-inch thick slices
- 2 cups of shredded carrots
- 4 tablespoons of crumbled feta
- 3 tablespoons of fresh lemon juice
- 3 tablespoons of extra-virgin olive oil
- Sea salt and freshly ground pepper, to taste

Instructions:
1. Preheat oven to 400F.
2. Place beets on a lined baking sheet and roast for 10 minutes until cooked through and beginning to caramelize.
3. In a small bowl, mix together the lemon juice and olive oil.
4. In a large bowl, combine the roasted beets, carrots, and feta.
5. Drizzle the dressing over the salad and toss to combine.
6. Add salt and pepper to taste.
7. Serve immediately.

Nutrition Information:

per serving: 209 calories, 16 g fat (5 g saturated fat), 10 g carbohydrates, 5 g protein, 2 g fiber, 356 mg sodium.

94. Mexican Quinoa Salad

This Mexican-inspired quinoa salad is a fresh and flavorful meal that will bring some zesty flavors to your dinner table. The addition of black beans, corn, and cilantro make this a hearty, nutritious dish.
Serves 4-6. Prep Time: 15 minutes. | Ready Time: 30 minutes.

Ingredients:
- 2 cups cooked quinoa
- 1 can black beans, rinsed and drained
- 1 cup corn kernels, fresh or frozen
- 2 cups cherry tomatoes, halved
- 1/2 cup finely chopped red onion
- 1/4 cup cilantro, finely chopped
- Juice of 1 lime
- 1 teaspoon chili powder
-1 teaspoon ground cumin
- 1 teaspoon smoked paprika
- Salt and pepper, to taste

Instructions:
1. In a large bowl, combine the cooked quinoa, black beans, corn, tomatoes, onion, and cilantro.
2. In a small bowl, whisk together the lime juice, chili powder, cumin, smoked paprika, salt and pepper.
3. Pour the dressing over the quinoa mixture and stir to combine.
4. Serve chilled or at room temperature.

Nutrition Information:
Calories: 184 kcal, Protein: 6 g, Fat: 1 g, Saturated Fat: 0 g, Sodium: 105 mg, Potassium: 262 mg, Fiber: 6 g, Sugar: 3 g, Vitamin A: 228 IU, Vitamin C: 13 mg, Calcium: 30 mg, Iron: 1 mg

95. Roasted Eggplant and Tomato Salad

This delicious vegan roasted eggplant and tomato salad is packed full of smoky, savory flavors. It requires only a few ingredients and minimal prep time for a delicious meal bursting with intense flavor.

Serving: 2-3 people
| Preparation Time: 10 minutes
| Ready Time: 25 minutes

Ingredients:
-1 large eggplant, cubed
-2 tomatoes, cut into chunks
-2 cloves garlic, minced
-2 tablespoons olive oil
-1 teaspoon smoked paprika
-2 tablespoons fresh parsley, chopped
-1 teaspoon salt
-1/2 teaspoon pepper

Instructions:
1. Preheat oven to 375 degrees Fahrenheit.
2. Place cubed eggplant on a baking sheet.
3. Drizzle with 1 tablespoon of olive oil and season with salt, pepper and smoked paprika.
4. Roast in the preheated oven for 20 minutes.
5. Meanwhile, heat remaining olive oil in a large skillet over medium heat.
6. Add garlic and tomatoes and cook for 5 minutes, stirring occasionally.
7. Remove eggplant from oven and add to the skillet with the tomatoes and garlic.
8. Cook for 1-2 minutes and then stir in parsley.
9. Serve warm or allow to cool completely before storing.

Nutrition Information:
1 serving of this roasted eggplant and tomato salad provides approximately 268 calories, 13g fat, 13g carbohydrates, 4g protein and 6g dietary fiber.

96. Broccoli and Mushroom Salad

Broccoli and Mushroom Salad is an easy-to-make vegetable salad that is packed with flavor. It is great as a side dish, or as a meal in its own right. Serving size: 4-6; | Preparation Time: 10 minutes; | Ready Time: 15 minutes;

Ingredients:
1. 3/4 cup white mushrooms;
2. 1 large head of broccoli, cut into florets;
3. 1 red bell pepper, diced;
4. 3 green onions, diced;
5. 2 tablespoons olive oil;
6. 1 tablespoon balsamic vinegar;
7. 2 tablespoons of freshly squeezed lemon juice;
8. 2 tablespoons of honey;
9. Salt and pepper, to taste.

Instructions:
1. In a bowl, combine the mushrooms, broccoli, red bell pepper, and green onions.
2. In a small bowl, mix together the olive oil, balsamic vinegar, freshly squeezed lemon juice, honey, salt, and pepper.
3. Pour the dressing over the vegetables, and toss to evenly coat.
4. Serve immediately or store in the refrigerator for up to one week.

Nutrition Information:
Serving size: 2 1/2 cups; Calories: 93kcal; Fat: 4g; Saturated fat: 1g; Carbohydrates: 12g; Fiber: 2g; Protein: 3g.

97. Kale, Beet and Cucumber Salad

This Kale, Beet and Cucumber Salad is a delicious, healthy, and easy-to-prepare dish that is perfect for a summer meal or potluck dish. Bursting with umami flavors, this salad is even better when voerlapping with a tangy vinaigrette.
Serving: 4-6
| Preparation Time: 10 minutes

| Ready Time: 10 minutes

Ingredients:
- 2 cups of chopped kale
- 1cup thinly sliced or chopped beets
- 1/2 cucumber, sliced
- 2 Tablespoons olive oil
- 2 Tablespoons lemon juice
- 2 Tablespoons chopped fresh herbs
- Salt and pepper to taste

Instructions:
1. In a large bowl, combine the kale, beets and cucumber.
2. In a small bowl, whisk together the olive oil, lemon juice, herbs and salt and pepper.
3. Pour the dressing over the salad and toss to combine.
4. Serve and enjoy.

Nutrition Information:
Calories: 104 kcal
Total Fat: 7 g
Saturated Fat: 1 g
Trans Fat: 0 g
Cholesterol: 0 mg
Sodium: 178 mg
Carbohydrates: 8 g
Fiber: 2 g
Sugar: 4 g
Protein: 2 g

98. Green Grape Salad

Green Grape Salad is a delicious and healthy salad that can be made in just minutes and enjoyed as a side dish or even as a refreshing dessert. This quick and easy one-bowl salad is ready in 15 minutes, making it the perfect last-minute recipe to serve.
Serving: 4-6
| Preparation Time: 10 mins

| Ready Time: 15 mins

Ingredients:
- 2 cups green grapes, halved
- 2 tablespoons honey
- 2 tablespoons Greek yogurt
- 2 tablespoons almond slivers
- 1 teaspoon freshly squeezed lemon juice

Instructions:
1. In a medium bowl, combine the grapes, honey, yogurt, almond slivers and lemon juice.
2. Gently toss to combine all ingredients until the mixture is evenly mixed.
3. Serve chilled, either as a side dish or a dessert.

Nutrition Information:
- Calories: 92 kcal
- Carbohydrate: 11 g
- Protein: 3 g
- Fat: 4 g

CONCLUSION

      Cooking and eating vegetarian meals can be both nutritious and delicious; this cookbook is evidence of that! The recipes in '98 Delicious Vegetarian Salads: A Cookbook for Healthy Eating' are an excellent resource for anyone wanting to make delicious, healthy, and vegetarian-friendly meals. From the simple to the lavish and creative, this cookbook covers a range of salads suitable for any occasion and tastes.

The diverse range of recipes enables readers to experience a world of salads and to mix it up with different flavors and styles. Combining traditional cooking techniques with modern recipes offers the chance to enjoy a wonderful culinary experience. There are many nutritious ingredients to be discovered and enjoyed, including a selection of vegetables, grains, and legumes. With this cookbook, you have the opportunity to create delicious, nutritious meals that everyone can enjoy.

The recipes require minimal effort and time to prepare, making this cookbook a great go-to for those with busy schedules. The recipes are also versatile and can be tailored to suit a variety of dietary preferences and restrictions. The vibrant photos provide inspiration for creating meals that are visually appealing.

So, whether you're following a vegetarian diet for health reasons or simply looking to explore and enjoy the delicious range of salads available, this cookbook has something for everyone. Use it as a guide to create tasty, nutritious, and creative dishes that leave you feeling satisfied. Set aside some time to explore the world of vegetarian salads and open up a whole new way of eating healthy. Enjoy!

Printed in Great Britain
by Amazon